Finding Joy & Peace

Living the Beatitudes Every Day

Marilyn Gustin

Liguori

ONE LIGUORI DRIVE
LIGUORI MO 63057-9999
314.464.2500

Imprimi Potest:
Edmund T. Langton, C.SS.R.
Provincial, St. Louis Province
The Redemptorists

Imprimatur:
+ John N. Wurn, Ph.D., S.T..D.
Vicar General, Archdiocese of St. Louis

ISBN 0-7648-0190-2
Library of Congress Catalog Card Number: 97-75917

This book was previously published under the title *Jesus'
Pattern for a Happy Life: The Beatitudes*, copyright © 1981,
Liguori Publications.

To those wonderful men and women
who have practiced
the Sermon on the Mount
and shared their experiments
with me

Table of Contents

Introduction

On a sunshiny day, a special young man was introduced to me. I knew he'd served a term in the county jail after a rough childhood. Now he was a struggling businessman and a Christian. Shaking hands with him, I asked the usual "How are you?" His face came alight. "I'm so blessed!" he exclaimed.

Blessed! He used that word spontaneously as Jesus uses it in the Beatitudes. To both, blessed means serene. It means joyful. It means contented. It means moving through life in a flow of inner well-being. Blessed means deep-down peaceful. Being blessed may not mean you have everything you want. But it does mean that everything, all the conditions of your life, will be fountains of joyfulness and tranquillity for you. If you are blessed, everything in your life contributes to your love of life and of God. Everything in the blessed life opens into beauty.

Blessedness, however, is not a quality we are handed automatically or magically. We must want a blessed life. We have to take seriously Jesus' explanations and hints of how we find it, of where to look for it. We must seek it, desire it, ask for it. Well, you might say, who wouldn't want such a splendid life? Probably no one —if we could retain all that we have "always believed" or what we "were raised" to know. But the Beatitudes and the rest of Jesus' sayings which Matthew collected (in chapters 5, 6, and 7) do require change of us. We call this beautiful and challenging collection the "Sermon on the Mount." It is the fundamental teaching of Jesus about life as it is possible to us.

The wonderful news in these three chapters from Matthew is that blessedness *is* available to us right where we are in life, right now. They are a kind of stairway — not primarily to heaven, but to heaven-on-earth, to blessedness in this our daily life.

Many people do not regard the Sermon on the Mount as a plan for blessedness right now. They tend to see it as a series of impossible commands, rules that only saints can live; or they see it as a reason to feel guilty about their failure to live by them. If we investigate the Sermon at all, it becomes an examination of conscience that is bound to show up our woeful wrongs. So we say to ourselves, "The kingdom Jesus talked about isn't practical for us now. It's for us (if we're lucky) when we get to heaven; it's a description of the way heaven will be."

That notion has been called "pie in the sky, by and by"; and, though it is a cliché, it expresses our usual view of the Sermon and the kingdom. But this is a misunderstanding. The Sermon on the Mount is for this earth, for our real lives in our actual world. It is a plan for us to live blessedly in the midst of everything. It is a pattern which — if followed — guarantees to place us firmly in the kingdom of God right here on earth. We must, then, try to set aside our usual view of the Sermon and let go our notion that it is impossibly idealistic.

Now turn on your imagination for a moment. If you were going to describe the earth to newcomers from space, you certainly would want to tell them how the earth works. You would describe the things you ordinarily take for granted: day and night; the effect of gravity; the weather; dangers that might arise, like traffic; customs that work for us, like eating food regularly; customs that might puzzle space-persons, like political conventions or golf. Why would you tell all these things to newcomers? So they would feel guilty that they did not live like we do? No, you tell them so that they will know how to live with safety and satisfaction in your vicinity on this planet. They can adjust themselves to what you've told them, so that they know how to get along in this strange world.

That is a good way to view the Sermon on the Mount; it is Jesus' description to us strangers of how the kingdom works, of the principles which affect its inhabitants. Jesus tells us how to adjust ourselves so as to enjoy the kingdom in safety and satisfaction. The goal is peace and security and joy, no matter what happens. How wonderful it would be to know that whatever awful thing comes into our lives, *we* will be OK!

There is, of course, a trick to this! We have already mentioned it; the plan of God which Jesus gives us for our contentment and joy does not sound much like what our culture holds out to us. Since we have been raised in our culture and are daily subjected to its overwhelming influences, trying Jesus' ideas may not be easy. Just for one example, consider what television tells us makes for happiness in our lives. It says to us: Be insensitive to others, and you will succeed. If you have any problems, there is something wrong with you. Be comfortable at any cost. Always be happy — happy and smiling. The material things in life are vital to your joyfulness — more important even than loving relationships. Success is measured in dollars or numbers of possessions. Be self-reliant. Be aggressive. Hang on tightly to whatever you have and whatever you know. Worry a lot about the state of the country and the plight of the world. Or don't worry — just ignore it and it will go away. Demand your rights. When you don't get what you want, fight for it. Above all, always be having fun; if you don't, you're sick.

If you think this TV picture of life on earth is correct and necessary, you won't like the Sermon on the Mount. It is quite different. But *it is livable.* It is far more livable than the world's blueprint for life. The Sermon is designed to fill your life with joy and peacefulness.

Now don't be too quick to agree! This book and the Sermon itself are not arguments with which you may agree or disagree. You cannot "figure it out" in your head. This book is a collection of suggestions and directions for experimentation in your living. Its theme is: "Try it and see what happens!" Then you can decide whether Jesus was right, whether it is possible to live in God's kingdom now, and whether the Sermon is any good as a guide. Take the Sermon in the laboratory of your daily life and experiment with it. Or treat it like a map for your daily journey, and follow it to find out whether you get where you want to go. Jesus came to promote the arrival of the kingdom in people's daily lives. In his teachings, he furnished traffic signs pointing out how to get along in that kingdom. He came to bring utter joy and deep peace. If this sounds a little new to you, look at John 14:27, 15:11, 16:24.

Do you want to experiment with Jesus in the kingdom now? If so, prepare to practice. Open your Bible to Matthew 5 and — begin immediately.

1

Your Part in God's Kingdom

The writer of Matthew doubtless arranged his collection of Jesus' sayings according to his best intention. For us, who want to practice it, only the Beatitudes seem to be in practical order. Since they describe both progress in the way and the goal itself, we will use them as our stepladder, coordinating the rest of the Sermon with them.

Before we look at the Beatitudes, let's see what Jesus thinks of us. Jesus is teaching human beings how to live in the reign of God, as he himself lived. Who are these creatures called humans? What is their place on earth? What is their place in God's pattern? We are asking, of course, what is your own place?

Read Matthew, chapter 5, verses 13-20. Now read it again. Here Jesus tells us who we are and what our purpose is as God created us to be.

Salt of the Earth   He begins by talking about salt. What does salt do for food? First, it is a preservative. It keeps food from rotting. Before the days of refrigeration, meat was salted heavily to conserve it for long periods of time. This method was widely used in Jesus' time. If he is referring to this quality, he may be suggesting that humans keep the earth from rotting and needing to be discarded.

That's quite different from what we often assume, isn't it? We think sometimes that humans make the earth a rotten place. But isn't it always "those people over there" who spoil the earth? Our closest friends and family enhance the earth and help create its beauty for us, don't they? Human beings who love us, who are close to us, do indeed keep life on earth from spoiling.

A second thing salt does for food is to enhance its flavor. Unsalted food is less tasty. The aliveness of the food to our palate comes from salt. This seems to be an angle that Jesus is mentioning here. Human beings add flavor or meaning to the earth. What would the earth be without humans? What purpose would it have without them?

Notice that Jesus first says, you *are* the salt of the earth. He does not say, *if* you are a good Christian, you will be the salt of the earth. He says you are now in fact the salt of the earth. The flavor of the earth is your flavor. What you are right now is the flavor you give to the earth. What you are right now is the meaning you give to the earth.

But if you give no flavor to the earth now, if you lend it no meaning, what are you good for? Salt is so elemental that if something goes wrong with it, it cannot be restored and there is no substitute for it — at least at the time when Jesus chose this figure there was none. Humans, then, are so unique as to be irreplaceable. If humans have no meaning to give the earth, the earth has no reason for being. It is our human capacity for meaning which gives meaning to the earth.

You are part of humanity. You are human. You, as part of the whole and as an individual, are the purpose of the earth. You don't have to change anything in yourself to make that true. It is true now. Just as you are, you give the earth whatever meaning it has. Isn't that a little awesome? Say it over to yourself, "I am the salt of the earth now. Whatever meaning the earth has, I lend to it. It is my own meaning."

This implies that your own quality is the quality of the earth; your own quality is the quality of your family, your job, your neighborhood, your parish — the world! In one way or another, you love the world, don't you? It is beautiful, full of wonder. Animals and trees and desert and sky and ocean — all of them add to the pleasure of human life. Even the feel of rich earth in your fingers brings satisfaction. A glance at the night sky inspires. You bear a love to the world.

What meaning do you offer to that world? How do you enhance it? Think about yourself a minute. And don't be hard on that precious bit of salt that is you! Have you smiled today? You have enhanced the earth. Have you touched a leaf gently, inquiringly? You have enhanced the earth. Have you hugged someone? You have enhanced the earth. Have you cuddled a puppy? You have enhanced the earth. What you already are, and the daily lovely things you already do, lend the earth its meaning and its flavor.

The larger helpful acts of your life also enhance the earth. Take a few moments to find and appreciate them. What have you done lately to say "I love you" to someone? Then consider your innermost self. You are literally made of love, no matter how blurred with fear that love becomes at times. Your self is love. Your love gives meaning to the world and everyone and everything in it. What you most deeply and truly are is the purpose, the significance of the whole earth. Ponder that a while. Enjoy it. "I am already the salt of the earth." That's a gift to you, isn't it? A little scary, perhaps, but a spring of joy just the same.

Jesus warns us about salt going flat, too. Is it possible for your life to get so filled up with fear and anger and guilt that your inner meaning has no salt effect on the world anymore? Rarely does anyone go completely flat. Yet, I once met a woman who seemed to have done so. She was so totally withdrawn, so fearful and so angry and so defensive against the world, that speaking to her was like speaking to a walking corpse. No contact with her innermost self seemed possible. It was a painful experience for me. How much more painful for her! She was almost like a nonbeing instead of a human being. Yet the day came when even she asserted her own meaning. Jesus' warning is one to heed. Vigilance is required. As we are now, we are the salt of the earth. But we must be alert to see that we do not go flat, that we do not lose our meaning. For if we forget our true meaning, we are no longer purposeful. We have no more reason to exist.

Light of the World   Jesus goes on to talk about light in Matthew 5:14-16. Again notice that he says, you *are* the light of the world, not you will be when you are something better. Right now, within yourself, shines the light for this world. Many have not discovered that light in themselves. Many perhaps feel that they have no light. Do you think Jesus was mistaken? Did he not know what he was talking about? So you must in fact be the light of the world now. Start to look for that place within yourself where light shines. It is there.

How do you begin? The first step is to be willing to find it. "Of course I am the light of the world!" you may say. But look again at yourself. As one tiny test, ask yourself how you handle a compliment. Do you squirm? Deny it? Refuse it? If you do, you are running away from your own light. One way to find your own light is to start saying "Thank you" and accepting those compliments with enjoyment. Another way is to ask a trusted friend to tell you what he or she sees in you that is beautiful. You will feel strange, but a touch of light will brighten your heart.

When you begin to show ever so little willingness to find your light, offer that willingness to the Holy Spirit. Do it consciously, deliberately. "Holy Spirit, I am willing to find my own light." If that is scary, do it anyway. Your own light is for you. It is the Father's gift to you. You can trust it to bring you joy. You can be free to enjoy your own light. If you are willing, the Spirit will rush to show you his shining within your own spirit.

Your light is not only for you. Jesus cautions against hiding your light. Who hides a light? When you walk in the dark and have a flashlight, do you stick it under a jacket? Do you turn on the lights in your house and then cover them with blackout fabric? No! You turn on that light so it can shine out and light up everything nearby.

Your own light, put within you by your Creator, is already turned on, already shining. You have hidden it with opaque material until you yourself cannot see it. You do your best to keep others from seeing it too, sometimes. Isn't that foolish? Why hide the light the Father himself gave you to shine out on the whole world? It is not your invention, after all. It is his. Jesus says your light must be allowed to shine out so the Father may be glorified.

Some of you may think of your light as a special talent you have. You may not know exactly what that talent is, but your close friends will likely know. Some people can paint pictures or write poetry; some can teach others or arrange flowers; some can enrich the lives of children; and some people are delightful for the sheer fun they are. Your talent is needed in the world — that's why you have it. Let it show. Enjoy participating in it yourself.

Your talent is a doorway to the true light that shines within you. Someone recently said, "I need *you* — not what you know and not what you can do." That person was really saying what Jesus was saying: Be yourself! Shine right out there for the whole world to enjoy! Are you afraid being your true self might bring ugliness to life? No chance. There is something beyond that layer of fearful emotion in you. Beyond it is gentleness, wonder, sensitivity, and a great capacity for loving communication. You do have these things. In them shines the light God gave you at creation.

We cover God's light in us with many peculiar qualities: fear, pettiness, machismo, spitefulness, jealousies. We cover it so well we can forget it is there. But we have only wrapped dark fabric around the lamp. The light still shines. We can unwrap it and it will bring light to everyone around us and to all the world in which we walk. That shining will create peace in our every day. The Father will be praised by other humans who see his light shining from our lives.

Suggested Experiments Do you doubt that you are the salt of the earth, the light of the world? Would you like to find out if this is true? Then try this:

Every day for a week, set aside 15 minutes to be alone and quiet. Relax in a comfortable chair. Just be there for a few moments. Now, look calmly around you. Look at the picture you like or the knickknack that a loved one gave you. Enjoy it simply and restfully. Sit. Enjoy. Do nothing. When you begin to notice a lighter, happier feeling inside, know that this is the edge of your own inner light, your own meaning. Appreciate it. Open yourself now to it and let it expand in you. Recall another time or two when you have felt this peacefulness in yourself. Be grateful. Feel that feeling. Let it pervade your whole being. Let it be.

The light within you, the shining which God placed there, is always for joy. If you will take the time to get acquainted with that feeling in serene solitude, you will gradually discover that you can get in touch with it almost any time, no matter what is happening around you. For a week, then, practice relaxing, enjoying, being grateful for enjoying, opening yourself to your inner brightness. Often remind yourself of Jesus' words: You *are* the salt of the earth — now! You *are* the light of the world — now! Be. Let yourself consciously shine with that being for a few minutes every day.

Law of Jesus   While Jesus walked our earth, he was often challenged by religious leaders, as well as by people more inclined to like him. His teaching seemed so new to them all. Some of his behavior didn't fit the rules and customs they kept. A continuing argument among them was whether or not Jesus had come to destroy their heritage, the law and the prophets from the Old Testament, and the way of life derived from centuries of experience.

When Matthew's version of the Sermon was written down, this challenge was still vigorous. By that time, Jews who became Christians were banned from participation in the synagogue. With such a clear split, it certainly did seem to some people as if Jesus had tried to eradicate their ancient traditions.

For these reasons the Sermon explicitly denies that charge in Matthew 5:17. Jesus wanted to abolish nothing from this tradition. His aim and his accomplishment were to fulfill it all. But he probably did understand this tradition differently from the way his contemporaries did. His understanding still holds true for our own time, for his vision remains larger and clearer than ours.

Read Matthew 5:17-20 now. Notice that Jesus does not speak of the little religious duties with which Jewish life was occupied. He speaks of the whole "law," contrasting the tininess of a Hebrew letter (the smallest one was similar to our apostrophe) with the whole heaven and earth. They belong together, he implies. The littlest and the greatest belong to the Father's grand design, the final kingdom of God. Unless every detail is fulfilled, the design cannot be complete; heaven and earth and law and people are all involved in God's tremendous creative enterprise.

So Jesus reaffirms the lawfulness of the universe, as we would say in modern terms. The universe expresses an order even if our minds have not been able to discern it completely. Jewish law was to translate this total orderliness into human behavior, that people might know how to live in the world, even if they understood only a small fraction of its workings. So also for us. We, too, have a place in the orderliness of God's creation, and we are responsible for the completion of that orderliness.

Jesus came not merely to make good the predictions of a Messiah. He came to fulfill the whole law in his own person, to live it out completely so he would express the perfect wholeness of the Father. He incorporated the core of the Law's meaning into his every thought and action and let it shine out into the world around him. He fulfilled the total law, as Matthew here reminds us.

We, too, are invited to fulfill the Father's law. Jesus urges no disregard for the law, either by deed or doctrine. He supports the law, though clearly in the Gospels he did not observe every institutional ruling. He expects his followers to support God's law, too.

Isn't it remarkable, though, that he excludes no one from the kingdom? Those who ignore the law will be small in the kingdom and those who keep it will be great — but they will all be there!

Since this is so, we need not be filled with worry and guilt in relation to the lawfulness of God's creation. We are searching for the reign of God in our living; and so, even though we may not yet keep the whole law, we still belong to God, to Christ. We can be secure in that belonging. We need not measure our chances with God against our behavior, as we so often do. There is no chance; there is only God's creation. His grand design is all that is.

Pause right now to ponder: If you know you belong to God and you know his creation is lawful and orderly, you can relax and be secure, can't you? When you feel secure, do you go right out and do ugly things? Well, it's not likely. It is usually insecurity that drives people to malice. The natural response from a secure position is cooperation with what we know.

Let's consider the "law" of gravity. We feel secure that the earth will not pitch us unexpectedly into space. In that security, so certain that we hardly notice it, we do not fight gravity. We cooperate. So also with the law of the Father. When we truly know we belong to him, that his rule in our lives is our home, then we respond cooperatively.

The last verse (20) in this section hints at how to cooperate: by being holier than the Pharisees. Over a long period of years, the Pharisees had become enmeshed in a complex system of rules. Many of them strove mightily to observe each one, and they expected everyone else to do likewise. They were regarded as the most holy among the people, because they were reputed to keep all rules. But here, no doubt shocking his hearers, Jesus says no. That is not enough even to enter the kingdom.

How is this? He says we can break a command and be part of the kingdom, even if a small part. But we cannot be like the Pharisees, the rule-keepers, and even enter the reign of God. Why the difference? Jesus is reaching for something beyond mere behavior. He is pushing people, as he consistently did, to look inward.

The Pharisaic law-keeping was external. The law was beyond persons, objective and not within them. But Jesus always pointed to religious practice that sprang from inward conditions. It is the inner self that participates in the kingdom of God. He insists that we turn inward, that holiness is a state within us. Therein we find peace. No amount of external rule-keeping can give us that inner kingdom.

Today, psychology recognizes that our inner state is precisely what we do express whether we wish to or not. Inner realities are recognized in a slip of the tongue, as well as in deliberate decision. Psychology supports what Jesus already knew: Our outward behavior merely manifests what is within us. Consequently, it is within us that the kingdom is founded and within us that holiness abides. No amount of clenched-fist rule-keeping can fulfill the lawfulness of God's creation. Only inner wholeness is powerful enough that our fulfillment of God's law can accompany Jesus' fulfillment. Entrance into the kingdom has little to do with whether we keep or do not keep rules. We enter the kingdom in our own inner holiness. The Sermon describes these inner conditions that enable the reign of God to unfold in us.

Reflections   Let's pause here to reflect on these verses. Consider especially the connectedness of everything: heaven and earth, law, humans, the kingdom and its fulfillment. They belong together. They form a pattern which we can see only partially. The goal of that pattern is peace and we are created to conform to it. Since we are part of that design, it is not difficult for us to fulfill it. We have made it difficult for ourselves.

Have you ever tried to use a tool for some purpose other than its intended one? Have you tried to pound a nail with scissors, for example? I have — and the scissors broke. So it is with us. We were created by God to fulfill a place in his kingdom, his tremendous composition. We are therefore able to do so; in fact, it is easier to do so than not to, for we, like the scissors, may break ourselves on a different self-set purpose. Jesus does not ask of us anything impossible in verse 20. He merely points in a direction we tend to ignore: inward. Just as the kingdom could not be fulfilled without Jesus, so it also cannot be fulfilled without you and me. No matter what the size of our part in the kingdom, without us it is incomplete. Since the kingdom is not somewhere distant but as close as our own breathing, we can move toward its fulfillment in us and our fulfillment in it.

Jesus did not present us, his followers, with puzzles. He wanted to show us openly how to become the kingdom members we were created to be. As we accept his invitation, our light becomes more apparent. As we grow toward his kingdom, we shine on the world more and more like he did and experience within our selves the peace that belongs to us in God (see John 15:11).

2

Trust
in
God

How blest are the poor in spirit:
the reign of God is theirs (Matthew 5:3).

This first of the Beatitudes is very much disputed. What Jesus meant by this kind of poverty is not always easy for us to grasp. The reason for the difficulty, however, lies not in our intelligence or in the cleverness of our scholarship. The difficulty lies in our pride. Let's see how that is so.

"Poor in spirit" does not mean that people who must scrounge for a material living are blessed. It simply does not refer to material poverty. People who are poor and people who have enough can be equally poor in spirit. Poverty of money can nudge a person toward poverty of spirit, but it can also nudge him or her toward bitterness and hopelessness. Perhaps the one advantage of material poverty is that it makes it harder to believe in one's own self-sufficiency. Although doubt about self-sufficiency may bring us discomfort, it is a big help toward the poverty of spirit which brings us the kingdom.

Yet, external conditions, however helpful or important they may be, are not discussed in the Beatitudes. They refer instead to inner conditions.

What does it mean then to be poor? Money-poor persons know that they don't have enough. The poor in spirit know that of themselves they aren't enough. They didn't create themselves, don't understand themselves, especially in the deeps of their being. Poor persons need and know they need. They need love. They need sharing. They need guidance. They need peace. They need a sense of direction and inner growth. They know they need these things. They are willing to see that their needs imply change. That can make them uneasy.

If you are in close touch with your deepest needs, you will reach out for God. If you are in touch with those needs, you know you cannot fulfill yourself. You will ask God to come to your aid. You will invite him to show you the way to peace, guidance, loving security, and all the rest. When you invite him to do that, you may be sure he will. As God responds to your real needs, his reign is established in your living. You are blessed. You experience the serenity known only by those people who do not trust in their own apparent self-sufficiency. You know the interior joy springing up in those who are eager to exchange their pride for openhanded dependency, so that God can direct their everyday lives.

If you are poor in spirit, knowing your needs and reaching out to God, you must then trust him to meet those needs. All of us are immediately aware of certain material necessities — food, clothes, shelter. Many people can imagine God giving them love, but cannot make any connection between that and God giving them physical sustenance. Yet, in a familiar passage about birds and flowers (Matthew 6:26-34), Jesus insists that God will do just that.

The issues for the inner life are two: Where is your goal? Do you trust God?

Where Is Your Goal? If your goal is material — a million dollars in ten years or even a new car next year — you cannot expect God to take over the material side of things. If you choose material things for your primary aim, it will be left strictly up to you.

But if your goal is God and your relationship to him in his kingdom within your heart, then he will take over your whole life and your material needs will also be met. Maybe at the last minute, but they will be met!

In Matthew 6:19-21 Jesus cautions against making the material side of life the primary interest. The material, after all, is perishable. It can be taken from you in your own home. But "heavenly," that is, "spiritual" treasure cannot be taken from you. It is yours forever.

Verse 21 is an example of how very perceptive Jesus was about human life. Your treasure captures your heart; or rather, you put your heart into your treasure and there it stays. For example, if you think and dream and plan toward a new home, your being is wrapped up in that house. If it should burn down two days after you move in, your own sense of personhood will be threatened. If, on the other hand, your interest and energy and care have been put

23

consistently into music and you happen to have your house burn down, you will experience difficulty and inconvenience, but your personhood, your *self* is not damaged because it is invested in music which still lives.

In one short sentence Jesus says that if your emotional and intellectual investment is in the material world, that can nearly destroy you when your world falls apart. But if your heart's investment is in spiritual qualities, you are on solid ground. Spiritual qualities last. No matter what happens materially to you, *you* will last because you have put your *self* into lasting qualities.

Notice how freely Jesus offers this invitation. He does not say you *have* to make one choice or the other. He does not threaten you with guilt. He merely describes the situation as it is realistically. "If you choose this, these events can happen . . . If you choose that, those results can happen . . . Please take note that your choice will determine your state of being." Then he leaves the choice itself up to you. You may want to look again at Matthew 6:19-21.

That is what makes the Sermon both wonderful and scary. You are free to make all your choices as you wish. You are under no external compulsion, not even from God. You may do as you wish. The Sermon describes the choices and their results and leaves you as free as the day you were created in the mind of God. Every time and forever, the choice is yours.

Do You Trust God? Next, Jesus turns directly to the matter of money. He says it is not possible (in Matthew 6:24b) to choose both money and God as your goal. Then with all his articulate love he points out some of the reasons why God is the logical choice. You, he says, are more important to God than any other part of his creation. He takes good care of the lesser parts. Why don't you trust him to take equally good care of you?

Think about this. Do you really think God sees no opportunities that you can't see? Does he draw only from the limited resources you happen to know about? Don't you suppose he has some options that you are not aware of? Is he as limited in his possibilities as you feel you are? Surely God must be bigger and more able than that!

Why then do you not let go and trust him? Well, you may not believe he is interested in the maintenance of your body. But how could God be uninterested in his creation? Why would Jesus have bothered with humans if they were not infinitely precious to the Father? You might well imagine that God cares for other people, especially those obviously saintly like Mother Teresa of Calcutta. "But *I* am not worthy!"

Clinging to your own feeling of unworthiness is merely a subtle form of pride. You want to depend on your own earnings or merit. But no one earns God. Anyone who reaches God simply loves him and says a big, happy YES to what he wants to give. You and I can too!

Does Jesus say "Blest are the worthy . . ."? No. In fact, in the Gospel of Luke, he says "it pleases the Father to give you the kingdom" (Luke 12:32). He does not offer you the kingdom because you are worthy. That is irrelevant. He offers you the kingdom because he likes doing it, because he likes you and wants you in it with him. He is consistent with himself and not dependent on you. That is why you can trust him!

Seek First the Kingdom   The main point that Jesus makes here is in Matthew 6:33: "Seek first his kingship over you, his way of holiness, and all these things will be given you besides." Is this your goal? Are you even a little willing to make it your goal?

Once some friends were arguing against trusting God for material needs. They told of a missionary who had given her whole life to foreign-mission work. "Then," they said, "when she came home she had to live out her old age in a one-room garage and didn't even have decent clothes. She barely had enough to eat. And you're saying God took care of her?"

Why are we so quick to blame God if things don't seem to work the way Jesus said they do? Why don't we instead examine our own functioning? The only question to be asked of that returned missionary is whether she put the kingdom first in her life. Did she want the reign of God over her personal life more than she wanted anything else? That is a question only she and God can answer. No one else can assess her goals.

We can suggest this much: Being professionally religious or in service-oriented work does not necessarily mean a person's goal is the kingdom. One's goal could be accomplishment, for example, or status in the Church. Or it could be the earning of merit, the earning of a place in heaven. Human motivation is very complicated. Jeremiah recognized that 600 years before Jesus: "More tortuous than all else is the human heart, beyond remedy; who can understand it? I, the LORD, alone probe the mind and test the heart. . ." (Jeremiah 17:9-10). So when we see a stumbling block in someone else's life, let's leave the evaluation of hearts and goals to the Lord.

The question for us is this: When something goes wrong with Jesus' way of life, is it more likely to be God's confusion or ours? God's mistake or ours? When we turn on a TV set and it doesn't come on, do we assume that no TV can work? Rather we check the connection, fiddle with the knobs, or take the set to the repairman. But the workability of TV we don't question. When something goes wrong with us and God, it often seems easier to blame God or to underestimate his ability than to ask ourselves if something might be amiss with our receiver, our own heart, our own selves.

According to the Sermon, if our material needs are not being met, the first thing to examine is our priority. What is it? Jesus only promised that our needs would be met if we put first the kingdom of God, that is, God's sovereignty over our daily lives. Jesus says that unbelievers "run after all these things" — perhaps because they do in fact have to. But those who love the Father and put him first simply don't have to chase after material adequacy. It comes.

So Jesus says that you can now stop worrying about tomorrow, because God himself will take care of his kingdom people tomorrow.

Here are a few questions which may help you determine your priority and find how your present trust in God actually operates:

• Do you think God will take care of your pocketbook? Why or why not? Do you believe Jesus here? Is something else bothering you?

• Do you think God will take care of your emotional needs? Why or why not? Do you believe Jesus' words?

• Do you understand the kingdom of God and its goodness as belonging to your daily life? Or is it only for heaven someday?

• Do you spend a regular daily time in prayer? Is it consistent? When you pray, do you listen as well as talk?

Leaning on God   Perhaps, our trouble in being poor in spirit is that it requires trustful leaning on God. Dependence is not something we accept easily or do readily. Our society does not help us with it, either.

Once a group of people got into a big argument. The question was, "Where in the Bible does it say that God helps those who help themselves?" One person maintained it wasn't in the Bible at all, and the argument turned into yes-it-is-no-it-isn't. Finally, someone offered a $50 prize for anyone who could find it in the Bible. That stopped the argument, but it didn't locate the saying!

It is not in the Bible. Benjamin Franklin said it. It is woven inseparably into the fabric of American life and independent, do-it-yourself philosophy. It is good Americanism. It is not good Biblical understanding.

The Bible urges people always to depend on God, to trust him warmly and freely. The five year old's "I wanna do it myself!" is not in the Biblical spirit. It may be a necessary stage in our human growth; but, ultimately, if we seek blessedness and joy and peace, our saying should be "God helps those who depend on him." That may threaten our self-sufficient pride, but it is directly in line with the spirit of Jesus as we see him here in the Sermon.

If we put the kingdom of God first and begin to learn to trust, we will find ourselves following Matthew 7:7-11. We will communicate our needs and be sure of the outcome.

Whenever these sections of the Sermon are discussed by adult groups, the objection is raised, "But I can't just sit and do nothing and expect God to bring it all to my feet!"

First, let's visualize a continuing series with total dependence at one end and total self-sufficiency at the other. We live already so far toward the independent end that we have a very long way to come even to the middle! That we accomplishment-oriented, production-oriented, independent individuals will become too passive isn't likely.

Second, sometimes sitting down and doing nothing while depending on God is precisely the most practical way to handle a situation. I have a close friend who is very rational and independent and capable. She's a little suspicious of my religion because it doesn't fit her "reason." We were having a friendly controversy about this matter of depending on God. "I suppose," she said waving her arm in a big circle, "that you're going to tell me God will clean this house for me!" Well, the house was pretty bad. There had been illness in the midst of remodeling, the children demanded a lot of time, money had run short, and the house needed a lot of clearing out and organizing. We were going out to lunch, and as we went out the front door, I said (half as a joke, I admit), "God, how about cleaning this house while we're gone?" My friend laughed, I laughed, and we were off.

When we returned, a neighbor from several doors down was sitting on the front lawn. "Hi," she said. "I should have come over sooner. But I got to thinking a while ago about all the difficulties you've been having and I wonder — would you like me to come help you straighten your house? It's such a big job alone!"

How to Ask   How much have we missed only because we did not follow the advice in Matthew 7:7-8? Jesus' assurances are clear enough. But we tend to decide beforehand that God can't or that God won't, so we don't even ask! Apparently, (as we read in verses 9 through 11), Jesus' early listeners had a similar difficulty, because he tried to shame them into recognition of their low expectations of God. "Would you give your son a snake when he needed food? You don't treat your children badly; do you think God will not be good to his?"

But, some of you will be thinking, I do believe God can give what I need, and I do ask. Why don't I receive?

The answer must lie somewhere within us, deeper than we usually look. Jesus did not teach at the surface of life. He probed and penetrated into the human being. He understood how we are inside, how we work.

The next time you feel you have asked and not received, prayerfully consider these thoughts: Have you merely cried out to God for something? Surely Jesus meant you to say more than the words, "God, please give me so and so." Have you pushed yourself, seeking, to the deeper aspects of your request? For example, if you have asked for a material item, is it a need? Is it something the TV inspired you to want? Does it represent a deeper lack you feel? If you want a car, for example, is it because the present one no longer runs? Or is your request for status? Perhaps when you petition, you could probe the reasons for your desire, then seek the fulfillment of those deeper needs. The deeper reason may be more important to God than the thing you want.

We can also inquire whether there is something within ourselves that blocks our receiving God's gift. Once a priest received a series of letters from a lonely woman. For years she had begged God for a husband, and she demanded to know why he had not sent her one. Her belief in "ask and you shall receive" had been utterly destroyed. Her letters were full of bitterness, self-pity, and resentment. Was it that God didn't give? Or did the woman push away, by her negative emotions, the very relationship she wanted? If we are not receiving what we ask, then where must the blockage be?

The last verse (11) of this paragraph reassures us that God is good and that he will give us all good things. Reassurance is necessary, because we lack confidence in God's goodness and especially in his goodness to *us*. If we did trust him, wouldn't we *expect* to receive from him? Wouldn't we eagerly anticipate his response, like a child wondering how and when it would come and how beautiful it would be? If we expect his response, we have removed one obstacle to our receiving his gifts. We have opened our inner selves to receiving. We are not asking with our mouths and refusing with our minds. If we do that, our minds will always win out over our words!

In all this, however, the most important question is our total orientation. Do we want the kingdom of God in our lives more than we want anything else? Don't be too quick to give the "right" religious answer. Look long enough to find your own actual position. Then push a bit deeper. If we say we want him to rule our lives, have we accepted that reign of his? Do we live daily with hearts, minds, plans, decisions, and desires open to his approval, modification, direction? If our whole inner orientation is Godward, then our asking has power. If our purposes are the same as God's, of course we will find whatever we need for the fulfillment of those purposes. How could God pursue his own purposes in himself and deny them to us? If the purpose is the same in both, power is in both. Then everything we seek will be ours and every door we knock on will swing open.

Even the asking of these questions will deepen the dependence and trust which Jesus calls poverty of spirit: *Everything* is referred to the Father. When everything in our living is turned to the Father, that *is* the rule of God at work in us, the reign of God promised to the poor in spirit.

Suggested Experiments   Bea — a member of our Sermon group — was practicing the Beatitudes daily. She decided that for a week she would bring everything, no matter how large or small it seemed, to the Father. She actually worked at being dependent on God. "Here, God," she would say a hundred times a day, "what do *you* do with this?" When she returned to class the next week Bea was so excited! She said, "I've discovered that I have a God-Bea personality and a Bea-Bea personality. When I live the God-Bea personality, everything goes wonderfully. And when I live the Bea-Bea personality, it gets awful!" She had experienced the difference between the two by depending on the Father. That is one way to dependence: by taking every item of your day to God and asking what he would do with it. Do you think you might discover a kingdom personality and a nonkingdom one?

If your work demands constant attention, this experiment may be more practical: For a week, in the morning when you first awaken and again in the evening just before you drift off to sleep, offer the Father your dependence and trust. Your morning prayer might sound like this: "Father, I don't know what is going to happen today or how I will handle whatever comes up. But I know I'm dependent on you, and I trust you in every situation. Even though I may forget at the moment, I tell you now that I want your guidance, to fulfill your purpose for each circumstance." Then at night you may review the day briefly: "Father, I know I'm dependent on your love for the results of everything that happened today. I give each one to you in trust. I trust you to take care of each one and to give me fruitful sleep now." Since you expect results, say "Thank you" too. Twice a day, morning and evening, can start you off. Then you may want to add another practice or two: at noon, perhaps, or during your coffee break or just after you finish a task and have a free moment.

Do you feel yourself resisting such changes in your life? Rejoice! That recognition of reluctance is itself the beginning of poverty of spirit. It is a sign that you and God are still not as close to each other as you should be. So, your attention can be turned to another kind of asking.

"Father, I don't really want you — or maybe I do — in my daily life. Yet, I feel maybe I'd like to be different. I don't know where my spiritual life really is or what I need to change. But I am willing to listen to you and be led into more inner unity. I think I'd like to make your kingdom my goal, but it's scary, too. Here's all my confusion, Lord. Take it and straighten it out for me, please. Thanks."

In that very act, which you may repeat a few times each day, you are beginning to ask, perhaps with new honesty, for the kingdom in your life. The beginning of blessedness, of relief from confusion, of knowledge of God is already yours. Trust it. Follow it. Listen to him who promised all good things to you: Blest are the poor in spirit (now that's you!), the reign of God is yours.

3

Sorrow into Joy

Blest too are the sorrowing;
they shall be consoled (Matthew 5:4).

"The sorrowing are happy." That doesn't even make sense, does it? It's a flat contradiction! What can Jesus have intended by such a strange statement?

The first example of sorrow most of us think of is grief over a death or broken relationship. Both abound in our lives and the lives of people around us. Here is the story of one grief which deepened a man's understanding of this Beatitude:

Bill's wife had left him. She took the children, all the money and property. It was unexpected disaster for Bill. He had been content in their marriage. Bill's emotions turned life into a hurricane. He gritted his teeth with the pain of it. He was angry and he stormed. He felt scared of life alone and he fled into other strange relationships. Underneath it all was grief, a sorrow that would not go away. Sadness pervaded everything. At night he wept into his pillow. Depression hung over each day.

Then someone who knew this Beatitude suggested to Bill that he allow himself to feel his grief, and feel it and feel it. Let it *be* within him. Quit fighting it. Tired and almost hopeless, Bill did that. He let it be. He prayed no longer that it be lifted. He just let it be. Each morning on awakening he monitored his feelings to see if the grief was still with him. It was.

One Saturday morning, feeling sad as usual, Bill went for a walk. As he went along, he saw a child running, but at the same time laughing at some thought of her own. Bill said afterward it was like being stabbed — and the sword was joy. It just happened, clear and sharp and unmistakable. Joy penetrated his being and he felt almost as if he could fly. Thanksgiving arose spontaneously from his heart. The strangest thing was that this joy was simultaneous with his sadness. The sadness did not disappear. They were within him together, this sorrow and this joy. He could not explain how or why; he just experienced that odd combination. But from that moment on, he knew that mourning is blessed by God when it is let be and not fought. In time, his grief ran its course and departed.

Yet, the sense of blessed joy has returned again and again. Bill's security in this experience has freed him from fear of grief. Is he blessed?

Sources of Sorrow   Sorrow comes from many sources in our lives: death, desertion, divorce, disappointment. Unexpected change of any kind may bring grief. It may come with a sudden recognition that we have hurt someone. Sometimes sorrow accompanies our first steps in being "poor in spirit," as we experience sadness over wasted years or a feeling that somehow we should have known better.

However sorrow comes, it is always related to ego-desires or ego-expectations. Take a moment and look within yourself to see whether this is true. If you are sad, it is because you did not get something (or someone) *you* wanted. If you are sad, it may be because something *you* cared for was taken away. Or it may be that *you* have thrown away precious years.

Psychology has long known that whatever gets your attention, gets you. As you give your attention to something, you empower it and increase its grip on you. If you fight your sadness, you are strengthening its effect in your being. If you simply let it be, walking quietly beside it, sometimes turning calmly away from it, it loses its power over you. It may not go away immediately, for it seems that such things sometimes must run their course in life. But sorrow cannot damage you unless you encourage it.

Yes, sorrow, precisely because it is ego-centered, brings an opportunity to differentiate between I-centered emotions and love or joy. Thus one purpose of sorrow is to goad the mournful one into growth. It points to ego-centeredness so that one may learn that ego-centeredness leads back to sorrow. The blessing assured by Jesus is hidden within that growth.

If you watch within yourself during a period of letting sorrow be, notice what happens: A new self-awareness will come to you. You will feel the difference between the ego part of you that is in sorrow and the more real part of you that is watching. In that more real part of you — as it emerges from the welter of emotion — you will experience joy. Joy is native to your being; it belongs there. It is yours by the right of creation. The Father made you that way. The ego, on the other hand, blocks joy.

Growth Through Sorrow Many interpreters of the Beatitudes have understood "mourning" to refer only to repentance from some specific wrongdoing. While this may not be the primary intention of Jesus' statement, the sorrow that is remorse functions like other sorrow and leads to the same consoling joy. Here the proviso is similar: It leads to consolation if you do not cling to your guilt. There is a vast difference between bringing remorse to be healed by God and clinging to remorse, whipping yourself inwardly. That self-whipping focuses on the regret, on the ego. It feeds the sorrow, enabling it to cripple you. But if you offer the sorrow to God while you allow the feeling to be — neither fighting nor feeding it — it will assist your growth as any sorrow can. You will soon recognize the difference between ego-involvement in guilt and the freedom from ego in the acceptance of forgiveness. If you choose freedom, the consolation of his joy will spring up within you as Jesus promised. Repentance never did mean self-whipping. It meant, and still means, the recognition of wrong and the quiet but definite turning away from that wrong toward God's love. In such turning around toward the God of love, profound comfort is the only possible experience.

Jesus knew that the purpose of sorrow is to lead us straight to joy. Those who mourn honestly and freely will emerge into joy, because that is the way the Father made us. Jesus must have known more about human nature at its depth than anyone else. Can we not trust his insights about sorrow and its comfort?

Thus all of us know sorrow in living. If it is a happy (blessed) state, that is because it leads directly to consolation, to joy. How can we help it along?

How to
Profit
from Sorrow
First, give yourself permission to *feel* sadness. If you want to cry, cry! Most of us have been convinced by parents or the media that real emotion must be hidden. Yet, feelings remain a part of us, and we are unwise to pretend they aren't there. Grief is a feeling we are apt to deny, and the denial often takes a religious form: "I'm a Christian — I *shouldn't* feel sad at death." Nonsense. You are human. You will sometimes feel sad. Give yourself permission to feel your feelings of sorrow.

Likewise, don't fight sadness. If it's there, it's there for a purpose. Don't worry much about how it got there. It has a message for you; it points to something important. You don't want the feeling to cripple you inside, so don't fight it. Let it be.

Second, offer it to the Lord, just as it is. Don't beg to have it removed. You may want to ask once, but trust him to respond in his time and way. Don't beg. When you beg, you are focusing on the sorrow and not on God. By focusing on the sorrow you will strengthen it. You can actually prevent yourself from receiving God's response. So simply offer it: "Lord, my sadness is my offering to you today. I'm not doing anything with it. You do what you want with it."

Once offered to the Lord, leave it. Some sorrow is cleansing. Let it cleanse. Some is a goad — let it stick you. All sadness is for your growth. Allow it to do its work.

Suggested
Experiments
Watch inwardly. Note the difference between your sadness and the watching part of you. "I feel sad." Notice that "I" within you. Perhaps you can think of a bridge. You are on one end, the sadness on the other. The capacity to feel is connecting you with the sadness but not making you one with it. Visualizing this, you can watch your sadness from the other side, your side. You can see how sadness works, what it does, what effect it has on you.

Then choose, consciously and deliberately, whether you want to cross that bridge and join up with the sadness. If you choose not to, notice how it feels on your end of the bridge: a little detached, a little open, a little free. This is the you that can be reached at any moment by consolation and joy. You do not need to do anything to produce joy. Consolation is yours — Jesus made that clear. You have only to let it in. But if you choose to cross the bridge and join up with sadness, that consolation cannot reach you.

You may prefer another image. Imagine sorrow as a person: see the form, the color of the clothes, the way it moves around. Look at the eyes. Watch it sit down in that chair across the room from you. Quietly, now, ask it what gifts it brings to you. "O Sadness, for what did you come to my door? What do you have for me?" Then be still and listen. A surprise is doubtless awaiting you as you imagine sorrow's response. One person's sorrow even took off a mask and revealed someone else beneath. That someone pointed her to a completely new and beautiful way of seeing herself. She was turned around by consolation.

Does living with, instead of against, your sorrow mean you go around moping and sulking? No, you don't need to. Sorrow can be profound, but it need never make your decisions for you. You must give yourself opportunity to express it in some way (crying, dancing, painting, sharing, praying), but you need never give it control over all your actions. It is quite possible to rejoice in the midst of grief, and both are true manifestations of self. Sure, it's uncomfortable to feel ambiguous, but it's all right. Who has not laughed at a good joke soon after a funeral? It's natural — and the part of you that can laugh can also receive the Lord's consolation, always given when you are ready.

When sorrow comes the next time, try some of these experiments. You may think of others that work even better to ready your inner self for God's loving consolation. Approach your next sorrow with a sense of exploration: Here is a chance to learn something. What can it be? Expect the promised consolation. Comfort — and not sadness — is your birthright. Look for it. Wait for it. Rejoice freely and be glad when through its door you may enter more fully into God's peace.

4

Meekness
Is Not
Weakness

**Blest are the lowly [meek];
they shall inherit the land (Matthew 5:5).**

Of all the Beatitudes, this one has caused perhaps the most difficulty. Its most familiar form is given above, although it has been variously translated. The troublesome word here is "meek." Its English meaning has changed with time, and it has been interpreted over and over to avoid the apparent difficulty.

That difficulty, for living if not for linguistic scholarship, is that meekness simply does not seem admirable. It may even seem sick or destructive. All of our social convictions seem to disprove Jesus' assertion. Our culture insists instead that "blest are the determined, for they shall succeed" or "blest are the hardnosed, for they shall win profits."

I prefer to use the familiar word "meek." It's really a rich word when we give it our attention. Let's look at what it does not mean, as well as what it can mean.

**What
Meekness
Is Not**
First, what is meekness not? Meekness is not weakness. Here we confront an erroneous notion that is quite prevalent in our society. We tend to think that strength and violence are equivalent, while their opposites are weakness and quietude. Yet, if we look carefully into our lives, we can see that we want to strike out, either verbally or physically, when we feel threatened, that is, in a weakened position. It is a rare and beautiful person who can be calm, quiet, and gentle under attack. He or she is truly inwardly strong. That strength is meekness. Meekness springs then not from weakness but from the security that makes all violence unnecessary.

As being meek is not the same as being weak, so meek persons are also not victims. They may appear victimized to people who do not share their inner life, as Jesus did on the Cross, but meekness chooses the quality of everything that happens. Jesus, for example, could have chosen not to be crucified. His power to avoid it is attested in the Gospels (see John 10:17-18, for example). But he chose it as a way to his ultimate goal. Do you think anyone could choose crucifixion out of weakness? Doesn't it take strength to make such a choice? If he chose it, he is hardly a victim, powerless and put-upon. Or consider all the martyrs across the centuries, who have chosen torture and death rather than denial of their convictions. It is not the observer but the inner self that knows the strength in meekness, that sees choice rather than victimization.

Neither is meekness equivalent to timidity. Persons who say yes to all and everything, letting themselves be pushed in any direction, are not meek. They are weak. People who become doormats do not want or are not able to make their own decisions. They let people walk on them because they are afraid to stand on their own feet. If by being utterly passive they can shift the responsibility to another person, they often do so. This is an emotional affliction which needs healing.

Meekness is not spinelessness. The backbone of the meek may be hidden, but it is there. When you try meekness yourself, you'll know that without doubt!

What Meekness Is   Meekness is decisiveness gentled by love. It shoulders the ultimate responsibility for one's own life-style, one's own choices, one's own quality. Guided by kingdom principles, supported by the Father, meekness is freedom from control by any other human being, freedom to create the quality of one's own inner life regardless of any event. A taste — a mere taste! — of such freedom can be intoxicating. It is a state we can all eagerly seek. It is participation in God's kingdom of peace.

Meekness is creative acceptance. One sees meekness when a person accepts a difficult circumstance and then, by a kind of inner chemistry, turns it into creativity. Meekness happens, as it were, inside a soul. Meek persons need not be defensive, because they can accept what is happening. Thus meek persons do not fight back. This is not because they cannot. It is because they know they are too strong to need to.

Recently, a young man we'll call Evan discovered that meekness is simply more effective than fighting back. He was in prison, but knew a lot about living. Leading a therapy group, he was in close conversation with a woman. A male friend of hers got upset about the conversation because Evan was a convict. So he demanded that Evan quit talking with her. Evan paid no attention and went on being helpful to the woman. So the man slugged Evan, knocking him to the floor. Evan got up and, without a glance over his shoulder, returned to the woman. The man was enraged and hit him once more. And Evan got up and returned to his work with her, giving no attention to his attacker. The man was furious; yet, he began to sense that something was happening which he didn't fully understand. So he quieted down a little, still belligerent but now a bit unnerved.

When Evan had finished his conversation, the woman was relaxed and smiling. Then Evan turned to his assailant, who still stood over him, and invited conversation. The result was that he too was able to learn and grow in peace: *Two* people experienced healing. Evan felt a sore jaw was a small price to pay to help that growth happen. What do you think the result would have been if Evan had fought against his opponent? A brawl? Perhaps an angry woman as well as an angry man? And no one any better off than before.

Turning the Other Cheek   Jesus further illustrates nondefensiveness in Matthew 5:38-42. He refers to an ancient, familiar law that remains common practice even today. Then he definitively supersedes it. "An eye for an eye . . . but . . ." What he says seems to us to be the epitome of weakness; and "turn the other cheek" has become almost a synonym for foolishness. Even Church leadership sometimes urges the "right" to defend oneself, following the usual legal customs.

Jesus does not take away that "right" — *if* that's the level on which we want to live. Jesus is not talking about the way things habitually go. He is reaching out to the complete kingdom. He is not saying we have no right to defend ourselves. He is saying if we want to live in his kingdom, self-defense does not belong. Once again, the choice is ours entirely.

Let's see how Jesus applies it. The general idea is stated first in verse 39: Don't resist injury. Here again, our tendency to self-justification stands up and shouts: "But it's only natural to defend yourself!" "Besides the Church says it's OK." "Where would we be now if people hadn't defended themselves against attack?" "But he did it to me first!"

Actually, there is no need to justify oneself. Jesus is not accusing anyone. All that he is doing is pointing to a state of inner well-being that is possible in this life.

So, according to Jesus, physical attack need not be resisted. Instead the offer may be made for its repetition. "But that doesn't make sense!" we want to cry. "All it gets you is a good sound beating." Perhaps. Or it may, as it did 2,000 years ago, get you crucified. Is the body's comfort more important than the kingdom in your life? Or the body's existence even? You may give a resounding YES! You are free to make that choice. If you choose the kingdom's life-style, the body may be vulnerable. Jesus knew that the body is very precious and he does not deride it. Here, however, he suggests that the body is not the *most* important. He lived this principle consistently, so that we could see it through his experience. If he had avoided crucifixion, where *would* we be today? Better off without his Passion and Resurrection?

Give Your Coat Too   The next most precious part of life to many of us is our pocketbooks. We go to considerable effort to keep them full and are ready to resist any attempt to empty them. So, if someone hires lawyers and goes to court to sue us, we hire lawyers to fight the case. Our right?

Certainly. But this is not the way of the kingdom. Jesus says if someone demands your shirt, do more: Give him your coat too.

A story is told about Muriel Lester, an English Quaker and a striver after kingdom life. One night she returned home from a meeting and found a man with a gun going through her dresser drawers. Their conversation went something like this:

Muriel: "Good evening! Now please put that thing down. I don't like guns and can't talk with one in my face." He looked at her, so stunned that he laid the gun on the dresser, one hand still on it. "Now, how can I help you? What have you come for?"

Burglar: "I'm taking all your money, jewelry, and other valuables, lady. Don't be tough with me."

Muriel: "You must be in great need. But let's not tear up my whole house. Here, I have almost no jewelry, but my money is in there. You may get it. I'll collect the heirlooms and a few other things." With that she went around her home, removing all her material treasures from their places and bringing them to the burglar. All her money she also gave him. As he walked out the door, brandishing his gun, threatening her not to call the police, she said, "Don't worry. Your needs are greater than mine. I will not report. I hope you have enough now. God bless you." She then went to bed and slept in peace. Did she live in the kingdom?

A few days later, her goods were all returned to her with an anonymous note: "No one has ever been kind to me before. I can't steal from you." That result, however, is incidental. It may not always happen. Jesus' way is not a gimmick for avoiding trouble. It is the way to live out divine love and to experience God's peace in our own minds.

Do More Than Asked Verse 41 — about being pressed into service — recalls a custom of Jesus' time. Judea was an occupied country, and any Roman foot soldier had the right to demand of any native that he carry his armor and equipment a certain distance — which distance we translate as a mile. Naturally, it was heavy work, took a couple of hours in the often hot dry land, and it was hated as oppression. It was a pretty explosive topic for Jesus' listeners. To us he simply says, if you are forced to do a task, do it twice as long and twice as well.

Today in the United States, we rarely experience enforced activity, although some people may. But we do rather expect to be directly rewarded for everything we do. If the boss asks us to work extra hours, we demand payment, often twice as much. If our time is infringed upon by a stranger, like someone in need by the roadside, we look to be rewarded for our assistance. If our spouse or a parent becomes demanding, we often resist inwardly and do no more than we must. We may not have Roman soldiers, but we have others who seem to make unreasonable demands on us. Jesus says not only "do as you are asked" but "do more," and he doesn't mention any reward.

Give to All Who Ask   Finally, in verse 42, Jesus says to give to the one who asks — a beggar, an acquaintance needing a loan, the drunk on the street. To anyone who asks for what you have, either as gift or loan, you are to give. "But what if the person is not reliable and I don't ever get it back?" "But the wino will only spend it for booze." "What right have they to ask me for money — especially knowing how hard things are?"

Oddly, Jesus doesn't seem to be interested in whether we will get our money back or what way it might be spent or anyone's rights. He does push us toward absolute openhandedness with all we have. It's almost as if what we have doesn't matter. Generosity matters. Sharing matters. Love-in-giving matters. Besides, haven't we already seen that God knows what we need and will take care of us when we put the kingdom first? (See Matthew 6:32b-33.)

People experience great freedom when they feel no need for self-protection, either for their bodies, their money, or their time. If your provider is the Creator and Lover of all humankind, you can give away *all* you have, and your needs will still be met. That may not mean you get everything you might want, but you will be adequately cared for. You can give fearlessly. You can give when you are asked — and relax!

Think about this, too: When you fight for yourself and your possessions, does it bring you joy? There is a certain ego-satisfaction in striking someone who strikes you. But is there deep peace in it? Will it really contribute to your blessedness, your happiness?

Meekness Spells Freedom Freedom from all defensiveness is meekness. The meek are promised blessedness. The Beatitude, after all, does not say "Blessed are the cleverly defensive, for they shall preserve their goods." Jesus implies, rather, that if we are meek, God will preserve us in his kingdom.

Meekness thus requires a certain freedom from ego. One of our most sensitive areas is our pride. Don't insults arouse us easily? Meekness does not need to support the ego. It looks past that to God and sees no necessity to demand respect. Most of us at times, and some of us all the time, feel a deep need to prove our worth to ourselves, to those close to us, to the world. That need actually makes us quite vulnerable, because we feel we must be constantly alert. That is not meekness. When we are genuinely strong, our security is not based on proving anything to anyone. Then there is no need to defend our pride. We can be ourselves, undefensive, accepting and open to all the world offers us. If we have no need to cling to our ego, we can be free. We can be free enough to be meek. That means we can be free enough to choose our own response, our own reality, our own integrity, and let the ego go unattended.

So, meekness shows itself as creative acceptance, in gentleness and tranquillity. It is based on security. Meekness is really leashed personal power.

Suggested By now you may be thinking all this sounds nice
Experiments but isn't practical. How does one find the security
that meekness brings? At this point, popular
psychology has done us a disservice. Most of us feel certain that if
others (parents, spouses, friends, siblings) have not or do not offer
us security, we cannot experience it. It's up to "them," whoever
they may be, to make us secure.

Remember, Jesus points deeper. The obvious is seldom what he
opens to us. Meekness is based on the hidden safety that is ours
when, and only when, we provide security for others, when we
make a safe place for others to relax and be themselves. What we
offer to others is what we create in ourselves and for ourselves.

Think of this as a circle:

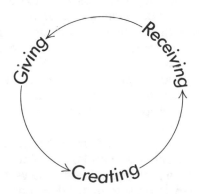

You can step into it at any point, with ever-so-small a step; and the
circle will carry you around until you have found wholeness. An
adult may not have received "enough" as a child. But almost every
adult can choose now to give. When you do, you're on your way.

So, if you do not at the present time feel secure enough to be
meek, begin to practice by offering security to someone else.
Somewhere in your life, you experience a secure feeling. Some
people do not scare you. With that feeling and these people, you
can begin to take someone under your wing. It may be a child with

whom you can play or an old friend whose insecurities you can reduce. It is not important where or how you begin. It is important that you do begin. Then, with the tiniest inkling of your new security, you can afford to experiment with meekness.

Danger   Another passage of the Sermon suggesting attitudes
of Anger   related to meekness is Matthew 5:20-26. Here is a
                challenge to our habitual way of life and to our usual
thoughts about ourselves. It stimulates a lovely vision of the kingdom quality of living.

The opening verse reminds us that we can be better than the Pharisees. Recall that the Pharisees were experts who regarded external behavior as the determining factor in holiness before God. Jesus does not say that outward behavior is not important. He simply turns us again toward the deeper, inner, spirit aspect of ourselves.

Jesus says that, according to the old law, murder is condemned. This is outward behavior. But, Jesus suggests, something within a person gives rise to murder — and there is the real danger. That inner something is anger.

First, let's clarify a widespread misunderstanding of verse 22. Jesus speaks of the Sanhedrin and of Gehenna. Members of the Sanhedrin formed the high council of the Jews in Jesus' time; the term is quite ordinary to his listeners. It does not in any way refer to some mysterious divine court. It becomes instead a symbol to indicate that anger and angry behavior do involve accountability. Similarly with Gehenna. Gehenna was the name of the Jerusalem city dump. As dumps always did before the days of landfills, they smoldered and burned all the time; the city dump was the disposal system for the community. Gehenna, then, becomes a sign for the suffering which ensues when anger is aroused. But it is not a sign or term for hell. These names point to an inner event and its consequences in one's own life, not to a future state.

The gist of these verses is this: Anger is dangerous. It may be dangerous to the person against whom it is directed, but even more, anger endangers the angry one. Consequences follow anger. They are built into us humans. They are not punishment. Jesus uses figurative language, as we have just seen. With a background of modern psychology, he might express himself differently; but his point would remain: Anger is dangerous, and it brings consequences which will remain until the inner result of anger is completed (verse 26).

Jesus is not here condemning anger as a sin. Feelings of guilt are not his intention. Jesus is describing the conditions within ourselves which foster or prevent our full participation in his kingdom, in our everyday life. If he warns us, it is not because he might send us to hell. He warns against here-and-now dangers that weaken our lives in the same way a doctor might warn us against hazards to our health.

Excuses When the subject of anger is discussed by adults,
People Use very often their first response is a certain
defensiveness. Everyone has been angry, and, of course, many of us want to justify ourselves. Justification sounds like this:

"But anger is a natural human emotion."

"Feelings are not moral — they just are."

"But psychologists say if you feel anger, you have to express it!"

"How can you not get angry when that child does . . . over and over and over again!"

"But Jesus got angry!" (This is supposed to be the overriding excuse. Of course, since we hear this from the pulpit almost every time the passage in John 2:13-17 [called the Cleansing of the Temple] is read, it's easy to think this way.)

After hearing these excuses in one adult group, Bettye suddenly spoke in a hesitant tone. "I agree with all the things you are saying," she said, "but wouldn't it be wonderful to live an anger-free life? Wouldn't it be wonderful?"

She had seen the point. Instead of justifying and thus clinging to anger, she had moved beyond it to a magnificent possibility. It was a flash glimpse of the kingdom. She no longer wanted to defend herself. She was reaching out for something better.

Answers to Objections
Let's reflect on the objections to Bettye's vision. *"Anger is natural."* Well, anger is ordinary. Most people do get angry. But even though anger is usual, it may not be necessary and certainly does not belong to Jesus' way of life. Jesus' way just might be better!

"If you feel anger, don't repress it." Absolutely right! If you are already angry that emotion must go somewhere, or it will sit in you like an explosive chemical and sooner or later damage you and maybe others as well. But suppose you didn't get angry in the first place? What if you so lived that there was no anger to repress? Now, before you shout "That's impossible," pause a minute. Ask yourself how it would be if you didn't feel even the tiniest twinge of anger. Wouldn't it feel peaceful?

"But Jesus got angry." Of course, no one knows precisely what Jesus experienced inside himself. But I think, when we look at him chasing out the money changers, we are not seeing anger in *him.* We are thinking, half-aware, "I would have to be extremely angry to act like that." Yet, John 2:17 says it was "zeal" that motivated Jesus. I believe Jesus was whole, completely, emotionally integrated. If he warns against anger, and then acts seemingly inconsistently, I want to look further. In my own life I know there are few actions that intense which are not anger-motivated. I would have to be almost out of control with anger to do what he did that day in the Temple. But then, do I care that much about truth? Am I as unwilling to compromise with evil as Jesus was? Do I put myself on the line to express strongly and unequivocally what I know?

Notice, too, that Jesus didn't hurt anyone. He upset everything but attacked no person. Reread the passage if you are uncertain (John 2:13-17). He acted out of conviction so profound, so dedicated to truth, that we don't know even how that would feel. Further, I must confess, if Jesus were an angry man, I would have doubts about giving him my total allegiance, because anger is frightening, and love and fear don't go together. Jesus didn't *need* to be angry. His dedication to the Father was strong enough to motivate any action he might take. He was powerful enough without anger.

Your Reasons for Anger Let's look together now at the underlying reasons for anger. First, take a piece of paper and make your own list: Why do you get angry? What makes you mad? When your list is complete, classify your reasons under one of the following:

- I get angry because I am hurt.
- I get angry because I am afraid.
- I get angry because I didn't get my own way (frustration, etc.).
- I get angry at injustice done to someone else.

If you think carefully and honestly, you will find that all the basic reasons for your anger can be reduced to one of these four.

Now suppose, just for the moment, that you are as firmly rooted in love as Jesus was, that your security and life-style and your thoughts are love-directed, that loving literally sustains you. With that in mind, let's look again at those four reasons for anger:

Hurt: If you are so rooted in love that all your concern is for the other person, need hurt make you angry? Can you not bear pain for love's sake?

Fear: Love and fear cannot exist in a human being to the same degree at the same moment. Biologically, for one thing, they trigger opposite chemical responses. If your love is reaching out to another, deeply and sincerely, fear simply does not enter. When you are not afraid, you need not be angry — right?

Your own way: Well, if you seriously love all people in a given situation . . . You can answer this one yourself!

The pain of others: This is the trickiest and the one most likely to be kept as justification for anger. If your love is like Jesus' love, you can reach out for the goodness in both the hurt person and the hurtful one. That's perhaps the biggest challenge — to look lovingly beyond the hurtfulness to the need underneath it. But when you do that, you will not need the anger, will you?

If you are utterly rooted in love and filled with love and motivated by love, anger will not even arise. If you can catch a vision of how peaceful and warm your own life could be then, anger will seem an undesirable substitute!

All Anger Is Dangerous   Notice this too: Jesus does not say that "unjustified anger" is dangerous and "justified anger" (righteous indignation) is not dangerous. All anger is dangerous because of its consequences for all concerned.

One such danger is physical. Anger stimulates chemical changes in the body which very quickly become poison. Stress-diseases like high blood pressure are anger-related. Many doctors insist that most types of arthritis are started by anger. Anger weakens the body and makes it susceptible to breakdown or disease. If you have ever really exploded, recall how tired you felt afterwards. Some evidence even indicates that cancer may be anger-related.

Anger poisons not only your body but also your emotional life. It can lead to depression, to increased defensiveness, to tensions, and even to more fear. Anger disturbs your personal relationships. You know how that works in your own life. Jesus remarks directly on this in verse 25: "Settle" it! Or *you* will be in trouble. You need not take literally the figures of "judge" and "jail." But anger does limit your relationships. It imprisons you in yourself by isolating you, doesn't it?

Jesus was right. Should that surprise us? Anger is dangerous to us right now, right here. One reminder: If the anger is already present, don't clench your fists and fight it down. Once it's there its effects are there, and it needs to find some expression. But you may seek to root yourself firmly and safely in love and thus reduce your propensity to anger. Then repression will not threaten you, because there will be nothing to repress.

You can be anger free! When you are, others will also be freer. In the true spirit of the Sermon, Bettye, who saw how lovely her life would be without anger, went home from the group to practice. A week later, she returned with the happy news that not only had she not been angry but "there was no anger at all in my home this week!" Everybody was friendly, conflicts were worked out, and they all enjoyed themselves — without anger. It can be done.

Meekness has no need for anger. Meekness is rooted in the security of loving. For the meek person, acceptance of what is opens the door to fullness of loving. In that growth toward fullness, anger finds no place. The felt need for it is gone. In its place is assurance, calmness, strength. All that can be yours. Sound good?

Inheritance of the Meek   What does it mean to "inherit the land"? It does mean that material things will be provided as you need them. But if Jesus is consistent, it goes deeper than that also. Again he aims at an inner situation. When you are meek you accept circumstances and make them creative for yourself; you live free of anger, free also from needing to resist attempts to injure you or to rob you of your possessions. In meekness you experience an inner restfulness and a growing expansiveness. You feel easy. Tensions and anxieties about circumstances or other peoples' actions or demands fade away. You become strong enough in love to loosen yourself from these cares. You can and will hold your days lightly. You fear nothing, because you choose the quality of your life in all events. Your security is in loving God, and no one and nothing can take that from you. Your inner self becomes like a calm, broad space where you find peace in your being. That inner tranquillity is your inheritance when you live in meekness.

In Matthew 5:48 Jesus urges upon us, of all things, perfection. Since we have traditionally regarded perfection as a life that is mistake-free, we've dismissed this verse as impossible, or we've tried to reinterpret it. Yet, it seems that perfection, like the rest of Jesus' guidelines, refers to an inner state: clarity of intention. It must spring from deep within us, and I think it begins with meekness. If we are even a bit meek, a certain perfection of desire for the kingdom is at work in us and will grow. Perfection may be thought of as something original within us, part or all of God's image in us, not lost to us but merely covered over and forgotten.

Meekness begins to clear away the debris that has covered our perfection: anger, defensiveness, clinging attitudes filled with anxiety, reconciled events that still rankle, determination to "pay back" what has happened to us. If these are stripped away, even slowly, we may be able to see beneath them the edge of that bright perfection put in us by God.

Suggested Experiments Let's experiment to see if we can remove the debris. Here are some suggestions. Others will occur to you as your practice grows; but, for the present, use the following procedure:

1. RECALL: Recall a recent incident in which you became angry or defended yourself. Remember exactly how it happened. Try to

remember what was said, done, and especially what you felt. Try to remember that flash of time between the provocation and your angry or defensive response. What did you feel in that moment?

2. RE-CHOOSE: Consider options now. What other possibilities were there? For example, you might have chosen to say "That makes me feel hurt" instead of lashing out. Or you might have taken a moment to ask if you really needed to defend your *self* or only your pride. Or you might have chosen to depart from the situation if you were frightened. You can think of other options. When you have several in mind, choose the one you think most interesting or worth a try.

3. RE-PLAY: Imagine the incident as a film you are watching. Rerun it now in your mind's eye. When you get to the crucial moment, stop the film and insert your new choice. Imagine how the incident might have been continued with your new choice in it. Let the new images run to their completion.

4. RE-FEEL: Recalling how you felt after that first incident, ask yourself how you feel now with the new choice and new direction from your replay. Give yourself a few moments to let these new feelings sink in.

5. LOOK AHEAD: What kind of feelings do you want the next time a similar incident occurs? Can you practice your choices now, so that next time you can choose them in action?

It is important in this exercise (and in all your new learning) that you do *not* say to yourself "I *should* have. . ." That will only make you feel guilty. It will complicate your new response unnecessarily. Say to yourself instead, "I prefer next time to . . . ."

You may want to do this exercise several times with different kinds of incidents or different kinds of feelings (pain, frustration, fear, etc.)

Another practice for growth in meekness is to share with another person your memories and your desire to change. That person can often point out what you don't see clearly or might even remind you of your own goals. Sometimes sharing helps to strengthen your efforts and to remember them when they are most needed.

Prayer with Scripture will also assist you in your growth in powerful meekness. For example, reflect on the Passion in John's Gospel (chapters 18-19). Is Jesus angry? Is he resistive? Does he go the extra mile? Is he clearly expressive of who he is? Live with these chapters for a few days. Don't concentrate on Jesus' suffering this time. Do notice how his own meekness becomes majesty. Pray with it. Feel with it. Ask the Holy Spirit to train you in meekness so that you become strong and peace-filled as Jesus was.

5

How Much Do You Want Holiness?

**Blest are those who hunger and thirst for holiness;
they shall have their fill (Matthew 5:6).**

This is our next Beatitude: Blissful are those who want holiness; it will be theirs. Jesus talks about hungering and thirsting for holiness. That's considerably more than a pious Sunday morning wish, isn't it?

Once I heard a vivid lecture about the early monks and nuns who left all they had, went into the barren desert, and lived in semi-isolation to become holy, to become fit for God. They made their living by braiding baskets from palm leaves; they spoke to one another rarely; they were alone for weeks at a time; they carried all their water, sometimes as far as ten miles; they imposed difficult disciplines on their bodies. As I listened, a realization suddenly struck me, and I turned to my neighbor to whisper, "I have never wanted *anything* that much!" He, a priest, shook his head, "Me, neither."

We live in a world which has somehow narrowed our desires, made them powerless. Our capacity to desire deeply has been stunted. The grand goals, the great aims often elude us. Yet, all of us who are attracted to Jesus Christ have before us the grandest challenge and opportunity possible: to live in his reign, to become like him.

Jesus offers no instant course in holiness. He offers no snap response to our meager wishing in that general direction. Above all, he does not make us holy when all we feel is a vague guilt that we are not already holy — which is perhaps how most of us feel. Jesus assures us that holiness can be ours, that blessedness is promised. We have only to desire it. But we must desire it as a starving person desires food.

Recall the picture of starving people you have seen — their drawn faces, the desperate longing in their eyes. How much did they want food? Can you imagine being in a hot desert for two or three days without liquid? How much would you want water? How much do you want holiness?

Or consider it this way: What do you want most in all your experience and dreams? Think about that for a few minutes. It's the old question: If you had one wish . . . Is it something material? Is it related to other people? Is it intangible, hard to express? Is it holiness? Is it God?

And this one wish — how *much* do you want it? How much time, effort, energy, thought, caring, practice goes into it? There is only one reason human beings do not achieve greatness: They don't want it enough.

When it comes to holiness, there is a lesser obstacle too. Many of us have been taught that true holiness is only for saints, for heroes, or only for nuns, priests, and ministers. But remember when we look at saints or heroes we are looking with hindsight. Were they easily saintly? Were they always as holy as we now see them? They grew as we must grow. Somewhere within them they wanted holiness, and they wanted it very, very much. Their desire for it influenced their decisions. Their desire occupied their minds, changed their feelings. Their desire was an active force in their daily activities. So, of course they gained holiness and found the blessings of joy and peace that come with it.

Holiness is for everyone. It's for you. It's for me. There is only one condition — only one! We have to want it. Like hunger and like thirst we have to want it. Then we need have no anxiety, for the object of our desire will certainly be ours.

Desire for Holiness   Jesus, knowing that deep love of holiness himself, did not suggest that we could toss it off easily. In Matthew 5:27-30 he indicates what such desire might entail. Yet, he is not discouraging.

Note again that it is the inner thought that matters, not primarily the external action. The external is always powered from within. Jesus knew that the inner disposition is the reality; the outer action is only an effect. This is the clue to our capacity for holiness.

If we want holiness, we can fill our thoughts with it. We can ponder its beauty. We can consider its attractiveness within our hearts. We can long for its results. We can encourage every thought that leads toward the holiness we desire. The inward attitude comes first. Our attitudes create actions and circumstances like themselves, becoming visible in our lives. So when holiness is our desire, fostered by our thoughts, of course it will become embodied in our everyday living.

The converse is also true, as verses 29-30 reflect. If we desire holiness, we will be ruthless with ourselves in doing away with anything that stands in our way. Does Jesus intend that we should literally cut off the part of our body that is involved in trouble? Or that bodies are the enemy? No, for he has just made very clear that it is the inward thoughts that are actually our trouble.

Here Jesus uses the body as a powerful figure of speech. You will, if you want holiness, want to get rid of everything and anything that threatens your desire. Once, in a talk on spirituality, I was sharing my experience of reducing the number of my possessions, and mentioned the boxes of books I had given away. A woman immediately asked, "But why books? Why I would never give away books — clothes or jewelry, but not books. Why did you give away books? They're the most important thing in my life!" A friend of hers turned and said gently, *"That's* why." She wanted books more than anything else. There was nothing in those books which was bad in itself. It was just that they had gotten in the way of her desire for holiness. She did not yet hunger and thirst for holiness.

It's almost as if we must make room for our desire to come true. If our minds and daily lives are cluttered with countless things that either do not lead us toward holiness or actually do lead us away from it, holiness can hardly enter us. But if we clear out the attics of ourselves (or, as Jesus put it, cut off our right hand), there is space and possibility for holiness. Goodness does not force itself upon us. We need to invite it, if we want it. Those things we throw out may not be evil at all. For most of us, they are only distractions. But distractions are powerful if they become substitutes for our desire for holiness. When we take a trip, we want to get to a particular place. But if we take every side road we see along the way, we may never arrive. Just so when our goal is God. If we meander through all the distracting paths of life, we may miss him.

John Woolman was an 18th-century Quaker. He became convinced that he wanted holiness more than anything else. He was a textile merchant in the American colonies and a successful businessman — too successful, he thought. He began to see that his business was occupying more and more time and effort and thought, and that it was distracting him from God, his real goal. So he devised a plan. He determined how much business he had to do each day to provide properly for himself and his family. When he had done that much, he closed the door of his shop and recommended that his would-be customers go down the street to his competitor. He wanted holiness. Woolman made many similar decisions. His *Journal* is available in most libraries.

The Narrow Gate   Once again, Jesus did not assure us that holiness would be easy. He emphasized that it is difficult — so much so that many choose not to reach for it (Matthew 7:13-14). It seems to me, though, that we have a backward attitude toward that narrow gate. We think of it as a disadvantage. We may find it discouraging. What's the use of trying if it's so hard? But there is another angle we may take.

How much do children like Easter egg hunts? How many adults thrill to the idea of searching for buried treasure or a lost mine or a sunken ship? How do we respond to the explorer who hammers at new frontiers of accomplishment? How many think it would be fascinating to explore the moon or a new planet? In most of us there is a wonderful response to such adventure. Although, probably, few of us actually will, a part of ourselves would like to be among them, wouldn't we?

These are not Walter Mitty dreams. They are indications that we were made for adventure — adventure in the spirit, in the inner life. And *no circumstance* can keep us from it! For many adventures we might need money or equipment or freedom from family responsibilities or physical stamina or something else we don't have. But for adventure in the spirit we need only desire.

Somewhere within your reach, within yourself, there is a tiny opening. It is hidden, but there is a way to find it. That way will be rough, but you can traverse it. Through that opening is wholeness of life, fullness of loving, fullness of peace, fullness of joy. You can have it. It is your birthright as a human being, a child of God. God has not made it difficult. You and I have made it difficult by cluttering up our inner selves.

But you *can* find the way and get past the self-made obstacles. You can follow the path to the opening into life. That path is not wide and obvious, but it is there. It begins right where you are at this moment. Look for it, peeking out from beneath the boulders of distraction and mistakes. Wouldn't you really like to experience the wholeness, the holiness, of peace and joy and love? Do you want it? Do you hunger for it? Do you thirst for it? If you do, it's certain to be yours. Keep faith with that small opening to life and start to get rid of the obstacles, or build up your strength to leap over them. With your heart full of longing, go on to your own most marvelous adventure. Go on! I'll see you at the gate!

Suggested Experiments   Here are a few suggestions to stimulate your hunger and thirst for holiness.

First, pray. There is never any substitute for prayer. You may have to back up one step and ask that you begin to desire holiness. Ask the Father to create in you a desire for him and his kingdom, a desire strong enough to start you irrevocably on your own path toward him. Don't ask unless you want it — this is one request he will surely answer in the affirmative!

Then you will want to take some definite action toward desiring holiness. Invest something in it. It doesn't really matter whether this action is large or small, but it may be easier if the first act is big enough to be costly and public. Then it's harder to turn back if the going gets rough. This first step could be a public announcement to your friends. It could be giving away something that's too important to you. It could mean a change in your life-style or the way you do your job. It could mean a habit openly discarded. Whatever it is, do it openly to provide momentum to your desire, to feed and strengthen it.

Another way: Make some time to ponder the advantages of holiness. Here are a few starters: Holiness brings blessedness, blissfulness, joy; holiness is wholeness, at-oneness with oneself and therefore with other people and God; holiness brings peace, release from all fear and worry; holiness is a quality of life that frees you to love and be loved without hindrance. Turn your imagination loose. How would it feel to be whole inside, to be free of conflict and fear? How would it feel to love without the complications of ego-centered wishes? Is a blessed life attractive to you? In a quiet place, think about these things. Write them down if that helps you.

Another possible exercise is to list the present difficulties in your life. Then put beside each item you list, the effect of holiness, of wholeness. For example:

Today proffers	*Holiness offers*
Feelings of fear	Peace, security in God
Conflict with spouse	At-oneness with self and others Freedom to love
Confusion of priorities	Desire for holiness in the kingdom first
Worry over a job	Blessedness in every way

Consider the quality of life you want. For the moment, put aside desired possessions or travel dreams or recreational possibilities. Ask yourself what quality you want your everyday life to have. Seek in prayer whether holiness might contribute to that quality.

For what do you hunger and thirst most deeply?

6

Mercy Spells Forgiveness

Blest are they who show mercy;
mercy shall be theirs (Matthew 5:7).

Mercy will come to those who give it, Jesus says. This is worth thinking about because we all need mercy. We need it from God. We need it from one another each day. The most practical way to assure ourselves of receiving it is to give it to others, to be merciful ourselves.

Mercy is eager goodwill toward another person. Mercy embraces the whole person with a kindly attitude. Mercy does not ask if the person in question deserves mercy; it reaches out of itself to another. If a merciful person experiences a wrong, mercy is ready to forgive. Mercy gives gentle acceptance, full acceptance regardless of what the other might "have coming."

It's a good thing, too! What if you were held responsible for every mistake you have made? What if you always "got your due"? What if no one ever patted you on the back and said, "That's OK, let's forget it." What if God, who knows you so well, were not merciful but only gave you what you deserved? That's an awesome thought, isn't it? I for one am very glad mercy is available to me!

Measure We find hints in the Sermon about a merciful **for Measure** attitude toward life and people. Matthew 7:1-2 gives the universal law on which the mercy Beatitude (and many of Jesus' ideas) rests: What you give out will be what you get back. If you give judgment, you will be judged. If you give mercy, you will receive mercy. Verse 2 reads, "Your verdict on others will be the verdict passed on you." Verdict is a pretty strong word, isn't it? Do we pass verdicts on other people? On situations? We may not have been in a court of law lately, but how many times do we say "That's dreadful!" or "Isn't she terrible!" How do we react to people in the news? To our neighbors whose values are different from ours? To our family members who make different choices from our own? Do we pass a verdict? And does that verdict contribute to our own peace of mind?

Our group studying the Sermon objected to verse 1. They insisted that people have to make judgments because they have to make decisions. Agreed — but only within limits. We do have to make decisions, and occasionally they may call for personalized judgments. But we should not forget that we can also take our decisions to the Holy Spirit to be decided by guidance.

Let's answer our own objections by examining all the events of one day. How many judgments were we absolutely obliged to make? When our Sermon group began to look, they discovered they make countless judgments not at all required of them. Are we required to have feelings about people in the news? Only if we are going to vote on them. But the lawbreakers, the disturbed people, the drunken, the violent — is it necessary to judge them, to feel about them? Or how about the choices our neighbors make? Must we decide anything about them?

"But," someone once said, "it doesn't hurt anyone to feel about people — if you don't tell them, they never know." That is true, but it is not the issue for Jesus. His concern is what judgment does to the inner life-quality of the one who judges.

Once I stood with a Sister friend on the Golden Gate Bridge. We had been walking across it, but now we stood, along with about 20 other people, leaning against the railing, looking down at a body floating in the water far below. A man had jumped about five minutes before and the rescue boat was just arriving, too late for life. All the audible comments were compassionate, concerned. For nearly half an hour this dead man had the full, loving attention, tears and whispered prayers of some 20 people. Sister said softly, "I wonder if he ever got this much love in his lifetime? And if he had, would he have done it?" No one was worried that he had broken a Christian principle; everyone present felt only mercy for a man now gone. Did we have to know why or how? Did we have to make any judgment whatever? No, it was enough to care and to pray. Wouldn't that be enough most of the time, while we are all still alive?

There is great freedom in the recognition that we don't have to decide about everyone; we don't have to have opinions or feelings about every circumstance. We can let most of them go by. Imagine how that would be! If we do not have to analyze the motivations of every person near us, we are free to respond from the depths of our own life-quality. If we can simply observe, instead of evaluating, we can learn so much more. If we are not judging a situation, we are much more able to enjoy it. When we give up analyzing for appreciating, think of all the positive feelings that will enter into us and spread to other people too.

Conversely, constant evaluation of others makes for insecurities in ourselves and also in the other persons. If we have the feeling that we are under evaluation, it makes us uneasy, doesn't it? If we project that feeling to others, doesn't it make them apprehensive too? Since most of us don't like to be in insecure situations, why do we persist in evaluation? Jesus says we don't have to. In fact, it's better for us if we don't because the same measuring stick we apply to others will be applied to us. That is not vengeance; it is an example of a universal principle. When we plant corn in a field, we will harvest corn. If we measure and evaluate, we will likewise be measured and evaluated. Do we want that?

Wouldn't we all be much more serene without mutual evaluation? We might all feel free to be ourselves, knowing that we would be appreciated instead of judged. We can begin with ourselves. We can choose every day to enjoy and appreciate instead of analyzing and evaluating.

Look to Yourself First   Then Jesus goes on (in Matthew 7:3-5) to point out that those who busy themselves in evaluating others can't even see clearly enough to help them. Every one of you wants to be helpful to people, don't you?

That's beautiful! But Jesus says the first step to becoming helpful is to start working on your own growth. As you learn and grow, your insight deepens. Then you can help others because you see them as they are. You need not pass a verdict on their behavior. When you see yourself as you truly are, you know that your brother and sister are just like you. Then you can share instead of judge, enjoy instead of measure.

"Treat others the way you would have them treat you" (Matthew 7:12). These words of Jesus form the basis of his mercy message. This verse has been titled, argued over, interpreted, and psychologized until it hardly has its own meaning any more. Here's just one more slant on it. Jesus is not urging you to do this for the good of the "other person." To treat others as you would like to be treated is very practical for you, because, as we've been seeing, you will be treated in that same way. If you appreciate others, you will be appreciated. If you evaluate others, you will be evaluated. If you are mean to others, you will experience meanness. If you are loving to others, you will receive love. The reason for this so-called "Golden Rule" is not to make others feel better at the expense of your efforts. It is to create in your own life the quality you want. If you spread acceptance around, that same acceptance will be your experience. Who would not like a serene life? How do you think, in light of this principle, you can attain it?

Mercy has another aspect also. Being merciful means not even wanting vengeance of any kind whatever. It means total forgiveness. Christianity has one primary purpose: forgiveness. Jesus came that all might experience total forgiveness. Christians who want to live in the kingdom have no option about forgiving: It is the core of the kingdom life. If you cannot forgive or, more accurately, if you choose not to forgive, you cannot possibly live the kingdom way. To this there are no exceptions. If you have not been aware of the centrality of forgiveness to Christianity, look up "forgive" in a concordance and read all the references in the New Testament. It will astound you.

Obstacles to Forgiveness In Matthew 6:14-15 we are confronted with an extremely blunt statement: If we forgive others, the Father will forgive us; if we don't he won't. How can that be? Haven't we been taught that all we need do to receive God's forgiveness is to be sorry and confess?

Suppose we look at it this way. God, in himself, is utterly loving and totally forgiving all the time no matter what. His forgiveness, like his love, is unconditional.

But his forgiveness, though always offered, can have no effectiveness in our lives unless we forgive our brothers and sisters — all of them. This follows the same principle we mentioned previously: If we plant forgiveness, we harvest forgiveness. God is not a tit-for-tat God. Rather, he built into his universe and into us, his beloved children, a special principle: What we give, and only that, is what we get. It's like a boomerang. So, if we want forgiveness from God or anyone else, the way to experience that release is by forgiving others.

The kingdom of God is a kingdom of peace and love. No one *can* live there who does not forgive freely. Still, most of us, no matter how convinced we may be that we "should" forgive, find it very, very difficult. Let's consider why it's so hard.

To forgive, we must let go. That doesn't come easily. Nothing in our culture helps us learn how to do that. We are taught only how to cling, how to hang on, how to grasp. To release, to let go, is a skill we have not practiced much. It is necessary in forgiving.

A second difficulty in forgiving is pride. We like to justify ourselves even if the feelings we are having make us miserable! Our pride insists that the other person is wrong, and we want to keep it that way to save our own self-righteousness. But by keeping that unforgiveness in our hearts, we make nobody as miserable as we make ourselves. Isn't it a little insane to want that pride more than we want peace?

Another trouble is that our feelings are very tenacious. We decide to forgive someone; and we think we have — until we run into that person unexpectedly or until that same person repeats another "unforgivable" act. All at once our feelings are churning full speed again. We know it's not healthy to submerge these feelings, but how then can we forgive?

Then, too, we instinctively know that forgiveness leaves us open, and we feel vulnerable to another injury. No one wants injury, and it is natural for us to be wary of it. But we misunderstand ourselves if we take this attitude, because unforgiveness is actually far more harmful to our lives, our selves, our bodies than anything which anyone else could do to us.

These difficulties cannot be explained away. All the theory in the world will not make forgiveness easy for most of us. Only practice and the development of certain inner skills will show us how to overcome these difficulties. However, learning how to forgive is not an area we approach with easy confidence; so, before we begin some experiments, let's think about the effects of unforgiveness and of forgiveness in our living. We may need to bolster our motivation for this challenge!

An unforgiving spirit does terrible things to us. No one can be at peace while carrying a grudge or seeking vengeance, even verbal vengeance. Unforgiving persons narrow their emotional lives by negative feelings and experiences. Their emotional lives are not free but are bound by resentment. Unforgiveness breeds physical diseases — all those illnesses we saw earlier as anger-related. Unforgiveness prolongs the effects of anger in our bodies, weakening them and making them sick. Refusal to forgive is poison to every level of our person.

Learning How to Forgive   The results of forgiveness are just as splendid as the results of unforgiveness are dreadful. Here are three stories of people who learned how to forgive.

✳ ✳ ✳ ✳

When I first began consciously to practice forgiveness (and practice is the word, because I didn't know how), I was living with a group of people. I was brand new to such a situation, and it seemed as if every time I moved I got hurt — hard words, opportunities denied, promises broken. There was one man especially who seemed to make my life unhappy every chance he got. Only with help did I manage to see that I was hurting myself at least as much by my resentment as I was being hurt by him. Further, the man was not intentionally malicious. Later, I was to learn that the motive of the other person makes no difference to forgiveness. But, as a beginner, I was glad for my opponent's basic decency, even if he seemed terribly insensitive.

I began to practice forgiving him. I'd almost feel clear when he'd do something new! It was a struggle. I kept at it. Then he went away for about three weeks. When he returned I ran into him unexpectedly in the dining room. *Without thinking* I hugged him! He was surprised — but I was flabbergasted! I couldn't believe I'd done that! Today, some seven years later, that man is one of my finest friends; we share an ease with each other and an appreciation of each other that is wonderful. How much I'd have missed if I hadn't persisted when forgiveness was so stressful.

$$* \quad * \quad * \quad *$$

A friend of mine struggled long to forgive the people in her childhood. A parent who deserted, a parent who convinced her she was ugly and useless, an uncle who threatened her sexually, teachers who convinced her she was "bad." Why should she forgive them? They had damaged her and made her life painful. She was still battling, now as a parent, with those childhood leftovers. As long as she continued to focus on the injustice of others, there seemed to be no reason to forgive. But when she began to ask if anyone had ever forgiven *her,* there was every reason to forgive. She really wanted the forgiveness of God to be complete in her life so she could find peace. She wrestled hard with herself, and she forgave. Several years have passed since then. Everyone can see the new stability and serenity in her life. She is happy with herself and her family. Her communication with her husband has improved richly. She *enjoys* Mass! Asked what has made the difference, she explains that it was her choice to forgive.

✳ ✳ ✳ ✳

Sometimes the results of forgiving are quite immediately dramatic. A man of my acquaintance is the administrator of a small company. We'll call him Ron. He had just hired a younger man to be his assistant. Ron felt Dick would soon become very important to the company. He spent extra time and energy training Dick and assisting him to get started in the town. He invested care and effort in his new assistant.

For a while Dick seemed to do very well. Ron and he got along well and the business grew. Then Ron began to hear rumors. Dick had been having lunch with Ron's competitor. He was sleeping around, though married. He was spending company money without accounting for it. Ron became angry. Then more angry. He wanted to confront Dick, but he was so angry and hurt that he was afraid he would attack him physically. Of course, he could have simply fired Dick, but Dick was a man of much ability. If only he could reach him!

Ron — a Christian who wanted to do not only the obvious thing but the loving thing — finally discussed the matter with a friend. This friend urged him to clarify his own inner life first, to forgive Dick and then make the necessary decisions. That wasn't easy for Ron; but he set about forgiving Dick. He even took his anger to confession, for help from the priest. When it was done, Ron experienced spontaneous peace and gratitude.

Two days later, young Dick asked to see him. Almost without preliminary, he told Ron all the shady things he'd gotten into: trying to undermine Ron's position, the women, the money. He wept and asked Ron to help him put his life together differently. Ron had said nothing whatever to him. Forgiveness within one's own spirit has abundant power to change things.

One magnificent result which always accompanies forgiveness — as exemplified by the above stories — is deep peace of mind.

There is hardly an adequate description for it. It has to be experienced. No anger anymore. No anxiety or apprehension. Instead, a feeling of strength and adequacy. This peace is not static but flows into and through all the rest of the forgiving person.

Suggested Most of us do not need to be convinced that
Experiments forgiveness is a good thing. Many of us have tried
it and run into those difficulties we couldn't quite solve. For example, if the hurt we feel we've received was deep — like the departure of a spouse — forgiveness is something we would like to believe in but find very hard to do. Here are some suggestions for growth in your skill at forgiving.

a) On several successive days, take a few minutes of quiet solitude to relax. Simply let your thoughts come as they will for a bit. The chances are that several persons who remain unforgiven in your life will float to your awareness. Or you may ask the Holy Spirit to bring them to you. Then, remaining quiet within yourself, offer to the Father each memory as it arises. You may want to say something like "Father, I remember that situation and I want to forgive all who were involved in it, including myself. Thank you for forgiving us together. I willingly join in your love for me as a person and for each of those people." Then simply let the memory go on by. Tears may come. Let them. But remain relaxed. It is very difficult to cling to resentment or anger while remaining physically relaxed. Then, as another situation arises in your memory, repeat the procedure. Always stay calm as you watch it happen within you. (Note that it is as important to forgive yourself as others.)

b) Focus on your life, beginning with your earliest childhood. Again, be relaxed and alone. Recall those people who hurt you in your early years. Follow a prayer similar to the one suggested above. Move slowly through the early growing years. Do not try to recall your whole life at one sitting. When memories come of your being hurtful as well as hurt, forgive yourself calmly, too. If emotions surface, give them room but keep a part of yourself serene and relaxed. You may find some stubborn resentments and want to share them with a person you can trust — someone who will accept your feelings and assist you in your goal of forgiveness. For some people a pastor or confessor can help; for others a therapist or a friend is best.

Through these exercises, consider that forgiveness is a choice. It is not magic. It is not purely emotional. It is primarily *an act of will and not of feelings.* If your act of will — which you can make at any moment, under any circumstance — is sincere, you will experience an emotional release. It may not be immediate, for emotions sometimes take a little while to run down. But if you nourish yourself mentally on a diet of forgiveness and thanksgiving, while admitting that the emotions are there, they will slowly depart, even if the hurt is repeated.

You will want to be careful not to deny the existence of feelings, for that only causes further problems. Once you have sincerely forgiven another person you may be sure God knows that. An act of the will is a spiritual fact, a real deed accomplished. It is recognized with joy by the Father. You can share in that joyfulness by thanking God that the person is now forgiven, whether that person is yourself or someone else. When negative emotions threaten, turn them over to the Father and again give thanks for forgiveness accomplished in his realm.

While you are considering forgiveness in a particular situation, you may come to recognize that the situation itself is dependent on *your interpretation of events.* If you interpret them as malicious, you may find it more difficult to forgive. If you believe that you have actually been injured by a particular event, forgiveness may not come easily. But if the mercy of the kingdom is your goal, your unforgiving spirit is denying you mercy. So you may want to take another look at your interpretation of the circumstances. Was the culprit truly malicious? Or perhaps caught in fears and confusions of his or her own? Or perhaps really needing help and understanding?

Aside from the other's motive, ask if you were actually *damaged?* To help discover this, look at the present moment, not at the past and not at the future. Is the real present moment, as it is, unbearable because of what happened? Have you learned or grown because of what the person "did to" you? This is sometimes hard to answer honestly. But perhaps the two following incidents will help you in this area.

✳ ✳ ✳ ✳

Not too many years ago a beloved friend, struggling in his own life, said things to me that I found devastating. Having preached about living in the present moment in forgiveness, here was an excellent opportunity to try it out! I soon discovered that I was clinging to unforgiveness because of my pride. I did not want to admit that what had "hurt" me had actually been good for my growth and had not damaged me at all. When I could let go my pride, forgiveness freed us both for deeper sharing. That was rather exciting.

✳ ✳ ✳ ✳

A beautiful woman — call her Sara — has struggled most of her life because her parents were alcoholics and lived rather chaotic lives. They are now dead, but Sara had kept her resentment. When she decided she wanted to forgive them for her own sake, she followed this line of thinking: My present life is the best I've ever known; it is really good; my parents had some part in bringing me to this present moment; therefore, perhaps even their problems did not damage me irreparably but made a kind of contribution to my life as it is right now; so, from my present moment I can forgive them and even be grateful for what they *were* able to give me. Her release was almost immediate. She can praise God now for all of it. Very often, as in this case, kept resentment is a matter of interpretation, of looking honestly at the present moment.

As you practice changing your interpretation of events, you may recognize that if you had not first judged or evaluated the person or situation, you would not now have the need to reinterpret in order to forgive. If you learn to experience whatever happens with mercy rather than judgment you will come to know that you have not been damaged at all. There is nothing that you cannot turn into growth and goodness if you choose to do so. Then forgiveness *is*. It need not be cultivated and planned. This is the height of forgiveness: to cease to believe that the person hurt you and to accept the fact that — by providing you with an opportunity to become what you are at this moment — the person actually gave you a gift. If you have never tried this, it may sound crazy. But then — try it; you have nothing to lose but your pride. You have everything to gain: peace, freedom, love, joy — life in the kingdom itself.

Results of Forgiveness   When you forgive you may expect certain results. Very often people experience a great relief, like a huge sigh in their souls. That is one burden they need no longer carry. What a light feeling, what a comfort, what an easing of inner tension! Sometimes you hardly know how tense that place in yourself has been until it's gone. It's like a noise you've gotten used to and so are startled when it suddenly stops. Relaxation follows.

For some people forgiveness is almost like falling in love again. Remember how much brighter and lighter and sharper and prettier everything seemed when you were first in love? Forgiveness may revive a very similar enjoyment of living.

If forgiveness is sincere, peace and joy — those inseparable twins — will spring up within you. It may not happen immediately, as we have already seen, but count on it happening. If after several weeks you do not experience peacefulness about that forgiven person, you may need to take another prayerful look to see if your choice, your act of will, has been honest. Forgiveness is not magic. Sometimes it is easier to *say* "I forgive" than to bring forgiveness up from the depth of your being. If you experience this, don't be hard on yourself and feel guilt. Simply return to a quiet time and offer it again to God.

Always, from beginning to end of the forgiveness process, you will want to pray. Pray to want to forgive. Pray for insight into yourself. Pray to be able to let go. Pray for inner honesty. Pray for whatever help you need to grow in the kingdom's love. Know for certain that in your efforts to forgive, you are cooperating with God's most basic principle for living. When you do that, God and all his universe cooperate with you. You cannot fail. You need offer only your willingness; and you can be sure the learning will come to full completion in joy, because that is God's loving will for your happiness in him.

7

Your Top Priority

Blest are the single-hearted
for they shall see God (Matthew 5:8)

The word "single-hearted" in this Beatitude used to be translated "pure in heart." Sören Kierkegaard, a Danish Christian of the last century, said, "Purity of heart is: to will *one* thing." That means to have only one aim in life, to submit all one's living to that single priority. So "single-hearted" expresses the idea well.

Most of us think that would be nice, if only it were practical. It is easy to see how much simpler life would be. But we hardly think it possible in today's complicated society. Indeed, it may not be possible if we are thinking of material goals or activity-oriented choices. Any single goal would have to be large enough to embrace our entire selves. Jesus, of course, is directing us inward again. This Beatitude reaches for an inner priority important enough to be the center of our lives. If we could choose any inner quality as a permanent condition of our experience, what would it be? Think about that for a moment. Lay the book aside and ponder it right now.

I have asked dozens of people that question. Some say "joy" (in the sense of happiness). Some say "being loved." Most of them say "peace." Fortunately, we do not have to choose between peace and joy and love. They come inextricably together. We cannot experience one at any depth without the other two.

Imagine what might happen in your life if your constant top priority were the peace and joy of God himself? Please don't object that it's impossible in the world of today. You would be mistaken. Such a belief itself would keep you from experiencing peace. The increase of peace—joy in my own life in the past few years assures me it is possible. Moreover, I believe that peace-joy can become complete and constant, because I believe Jesus knew much about living that I am all eager to discover in my own experience. I hope you will come along, for I need to share.

What decisions would you make if peace-joy were top priority? Well, for a start, you might decide not to be angry. Anger destroys your inner peace. If you fell unawares into anger, you might decide to forgive, because forgiveness brings you peace and joy. You might also decide not to be fearful. Fear is almost the opposite of peacefulness, isn't it? You would seek ways of freeing yourself from guilt for the same reason. You would decide that pride and those ego-feeding mental conversations going on in your own heart are all less important than peace. You would let pride go. Even sorrow would have a different flavor.

Making these determinations begins to sound like quite an adventure, doesn't it? These are all inner decisions. You can make them yourself. When considering decisions about relationships or your job or your money, how often have you asked, "Which alternative will give me greater peace?" If you begin to do this, two things surely will happen: Your decisions will change quality; peace and joy will become your companions. For an experiment, right now think of the next decision you know you must make. You may already have been weighing it for a time. Don't worry about how large or small it is. Look at every option in terms of this question: Will this choice make you more or less peaceful, more or less joyful?

"Why peace?" you might ask. A peaceful response to almost anything will place you right in line with all the Sermon principles. But the best reason is given in the second half of this Beatitude: The person with a single direction in life will see God. How can God dwell in a heart full of turmoil? Only a peace-filled heart can really be his home, and only the single-hearted person experiences God directly. It seems that the only goal large enough to remain single in our living is peace. Every other possibility gets cluttered up in the living of it. If we open ourselves to peace first and always (make it our top priority), then God will certainly fill our being. That is love. That is joy. Everything else we need will come with that Presence within us. What more do we really desire after all? Isn't God the goal of our whole life adventure?

Advantages of Secrecy The Sermon includes a few tips for the narrowing of priorities to a single one: the kingdom of God, of peace and joy. One set of hints is found in Matthew 6:1-6,16-18. Take a moment now and read this section. These verses boil down to this: Keep your good deeds and gifts a secret; keep your private prayer a secret; and do religious exercises secretly. This is not a prohibition of public worship or of shared prayer with a trusted group. Why then all this secrecy? Because secrecy has at least two immediate effects: It is a direct strike at the ego; and it fuels your own inner power. Let's look at these.

Things which are generally approved, like religion and good deeds, always carry with them the possibility that we will do them for mixed motives: partly out of genuine desire and partly for approval and appreciation. Sorting out our motivations is not easy; we can seldom be certain of them. One way to help ourselves do such good things for love, for God alone, is to keep them absolutely secret from any and all who might approve or admire us. If no one knows about them, these temptations to a puffed ego will be fewer. That fact alone may be quite a blow to our ego; and if so, it is to be welcomed with an open heart, for every space formed by decreasing our ego allows more room for God.

What does this have to do with single-heartedness? Well, the ego is clamorous and complicated. If you have any doubts about that, read the theories of psychologists about how the ego works. Or take a good long, honest look at how clever and how subtle your ego is. That may take a little time, but as you begin to observe you will see. The complications of the ego-centered life keep a person in considerable ferment. If you want to experience God, agitation is an obstacle. You are looking for peace, right? If the ego is pushed out of its usual position within you, peace and joy come slipping in. Secrecy helps push.

Secrecy also gathers your own inner power. It acts like a magnifying glass in sunlight. It focuses your own goodness, making it more effective. No matter that it may be unseen for a long time. You may not always predict exactly what form that power will take. It might go into your own increased creativity or your capacity for love or a greater freedom to be yourself because of new confidence. But focused inner power will be yours when you keep good secrets.

You may have become used to depending on external things for greater power: money, political maneuvering, manipulation, control. But secrecy will outshine these and all the others, too, because the response to secrecy comes not from the world but from the Father who knows your secrets. Look again at verses 4, 6, and 18. It is only for the Father of love that you do the secret things you do, and so only he will respond. He will increase your power to love, increase your power to create, increase your power to center your life on him, increase your power to pray and to be single-hearted, so he may fill you with himself.

There is no way to prove all this by thinking about it. Like so much that has gone before, this principle can be demonstrated by practice only. Experimenting with it will give you knowledge of its truth. So try it! The next time you give a gift, arrange it so that no one, not even the recipient, knows who the giver is. Keep it strictly between you and God. Any good deed or religious act that is habitual with you, or even occasional, do next time in complete secrecy. Keep it permanently within your own heart, to prepare a larger place for God to enter in peace. Wait and see what happens within you. Then try it again. Maybe you will want to make a month's experiment in secrecy. At the end of the month, look back and see what has happened within you and around you. You will make some very interesting discoveries.

Simplicity of Speech   Another contribution to single-heartedness is found in Matthew 5:33-37. This paragraph is about oaths and their inadvisability, a topic which seems at first odd, as if Jesus were making a big issue out of a small matter. If we take it literally — "Don't take oaths" — we may not be in error, but I think we miss the main point. The issue is simplicity of speech and conforming our lives to our words or our words to our lives. Once again, Jesus leads us away from complexity toward singleness. How so?

Speech is probably the most spontaneous form of expression we know. We reveal ourselves when we talk, sometimes more than we realize. We learn about other people, too, from their speech. Speech can also be used to cover up, though a perceptive person may see through such cover. People speak truth and untruth; they share love and spew anger; they express tenderness and bitterness. In all of these, the person is revealed through speech.

When you take an oath, you use an elaborate form of speech which is intended to make your speaking more true or more believable. What bothers Jesus is the assumption that something more than simple expression is required to ensure truth. Jesus calls for simplicity in speech because he knows that no one speaks simply without having inner simplicity. A plain yes or a plain no is quite enough when it conforms to the inner actuality. A single-hearted person speaks simply and directly.

A person whose character is straightforward does not need elaborate insurance for the truth. Such a one keeps his or her word when it is simply spoken. That person is dependable. You can count on him or her. You know that when he or she speaks the words are true and will be consistently held. Such singleness is the integrity Jesus seeks in people. If you speak simply, if you mean what you say, you are growing toward single-heartedness.

Simplicity of speech reflects an inner calmness. Practicing it can help create calmness, too. It works both ways at once. So perhaps for a week or so you may want to be conscious of your speech, avoiding the flowery, media-fed expressions you are used to and cultivating the simplicity of a clear, reliable word. You will soon feel a vital difference in your responses, and your inner self will move toward new unity. You are taking a definite step toward seeing God.

Singleness of Purpose The other comments in the Sermon which refer to singleness of heart are found in Matthew 6:22-24.

These are placed in a larger discussion about the fundamental decision men and women must make — whether to invest more heavily in the material, outer side of life or in the inner, spiritual side. Jesus says it is not possible to do both, because the heart will be with one or the other. He talks about eyes and whether they are good or bad and (in some translations) he speaks of the eye being "single."

Have you ever experienced double vision or seriously blurred vision? If so you know what a disorienting experience that can be. You are not sure which image is real or where an object begins and ends. Your sense of physical stability is insecure because even the floor under your feet (four of them?) is unclear and shifting. It is a most distressing experience, since your sense of contact with what is solid is uncertain.

This is analogous to the spiritual state Jesus is describing. When people try to give themselves to two worlds at once, the material and the spiritual, the result is like an inner double vision. They cannot tell which is actual, which is solid, and their contact with reality is tenuous. Of course, since most of us are born into this state of inner double vision, we consider it the real world, the way things really are. Jesus calls that "darkness." We are not really seeing, he suggests. This may account for our considerable insecurity about life!

We can only see reality when our vision, and therefore our heart, is good, is single. What is reality? God is reality. So when the eye of our spirit is firmly fixed on interior values and that is in fact the single center of our attention, of course we will see God. We will see only what is real. God *is* what is real.

How can we make our eye single? When we choose the reality of God, his peace and joy, as our only aim, gradually we will direct everything to that goal. We will become single-hearted, and we will see God. Of course, he was available for us to see all the time; but, because our vision was blurred, we could not.

When someone says "seek only God" many of us hesitate. A friend said to me, "But I'm afraid of that." She was honest and spoke for many. Often, our fear is that we will have to give up something, or a lot of somethings, that we would rather keep. But in seeking only God and living his life, this rarely is so; for the more we know and love God, the more everything else falls into beautiful order in our lives.

Wouldn't it be wonderful to be at peace? Dynamic peace of mind is a worthy goal for all our decisions and efforts. If that is the single direction of our heart and mind and attention, peace and joy will come to us. Into that peace God will enter, and we will know that we do not need to be afraid of him.

Suggested Experiments   In your quiet times, ponder in a relaxed way what your priorities are now. Are they unified or are they conflicting? Try to sort them out. Take paper and write "peace/joy" at the head of one column and "turmoil/stress" at the head of another. Then list your goals in one of these columns, according to their effect in your daily life. Include external values, like a home, car, material security, etc. Include, also, the qualities you value in your emotional life. Some items may show up in both columns. Now ask yourself if you can move one aspect of your life from the negative column into the peaceful one. Even one crossover will give you a taste of how change toward peace can affect your every day. Try it out.

You may want to experiment with earlier suggestions, like secret good, simple speech, arrangement of priorities. All will help clarify your actual present state of being. If it isn't single now, know that all you need is readiness of heart to turn toward singleness. You can wait eagerly, in quiet certainty, for your own experience of God, assured to the single-hearted.

8

Peace Starts with You

Blest too the peacemakers;
they shall be called children of God (Matthew 5:9).

Peacemakers are creators of a special kind. They take chaos or conflict or unhappiness and turn it into tranquillity. They may do this actively. They may settle quarrels or negotiate disputes or write treaties. Or they may work primarily to prevent conflict. Some people are professional at these peacemaking activities. For most of us, though, the opportunity comes in the midst of our everyday living. Conflicts can happen anytime and anywhere two or more people are on the scene. The person who is practicing this Beatitude will respond to such conflicts quite differently from those who respond in fear or anger. Such a person will take immediate action to move toward reconciliation.

But something has to come first, doesn't it? We can't give what we haven't got. We cannot create peacefulness unless we are peaceful. As always, Jesus points to the inner condition. That is why the peacemakers are found only near the end of the Beatitudes. The one who spreads peace is the one who lives serenely. Oh yes, someone may negotiate an agreement without inner peace. But that agreement is only the outward symptom of the conflict within the people who are fighting. A real peacemaker must know how to quiet that inner conflict. This is possible only when the interior life is tranquil.

All of us have met at least one truly peace-filled human being. Wasn't it wonderful to be near him or her? Wouldn't it be wonderful to have that atmosphere in your own home? Didn't you want to heap gratitude on the person whose peace brought you closer to your own peace?

How do you become such a peaceful person and then a maker of peace? You have been moving toward this goal all through your experiments with the Sermon. Living the principles of the Sermon leads straight to inner peace, to a calm outlook on all around you, indeed, on all of life. All you really need now is to be what you have learned, living each Beatitude to the hilt. The deeper your own peace is, the stronger its effect on other people. In fact, you can hardly keep from being a peacemaker once you have found the inner peace that is your own birthright. You will spread it to other hearts whether you try to or not.

Share Your Peace Once we begin to practice peacemaking directly, however, there are certain pitfalls to be avoided. One is mentioned in a verse which itself has been a pitfall for many of us. (Read Matthew 7:6.) We don't want to call anyone a swine! And in Jesus' time dogs were just as bad, being scavengers and rarely pets. Of course, these are figures of speech. Jesus is saying, "Don't be stupid with those things that are holy and precious to you."

In a way, this is common sense. If you have a vulnerable place in you, either a pain or a particular happiness, you may desire to share it; but you know that some people would laugh at you, or scoff. Perhaps only a few, or even only one, would listen to you and understand that pain or that loveliness. You already have a natural reluctance to expose what is important but vulnerable to any negative reaction.

At the same time, who does not enjoy sharing excitement over wonderful experiences or new ideas or situations or people? You may want to begin with the first person you see. And you may get cold water thrown on you! That's hard enough when the matter is relatively small. But if it is the holiness within you that you are just discovering and fostering, indiscriminate exposure can be harmful. It may set you back in your growth or frighten you out of sharing at all. You may look on this as a learning experience, but would you pull the legs out from under a baby learning to walk? Why, then, put yourself in a position to have your new spiritual legs pulled from under you?

If you are sharing holiness and peace and your precious insights and creativity, Jesus implies, be a little aware that not all people are ready for you. As you grow stronger, your need for caution will decrease. Until then, don't be stupid!

Share with Care How can you know with whom to share? (Look at Matthew 7:15-20.) You will recognize false prophets "by their deeds." Have you ever noticed that Jesus seldom seems to be in a hurry? It takes time to discover the truth about a person's character even as it does to wait and see what fruit a tree will bear. Jesus advises watchfulness to see what you can learn about people. When certain choices are made, take a loving look at what develops. When certain actions are complete, wait to see their consequences. Often you can preestimate a person's response to what you have to share.

But being loving does not mean you have to be gullible. Nor does freedom from judgment mean you give yourself over to those who are not ready for what you have to offer. Wait. Observe. Be patient and keep caring. Don't believe automatically all those who make great claims for themselves. Look first at the results or fruits of their labors.

But be careful that you do not begin subtly to pass judgment; for remember, you will be judged likewise. Your character will also be revealed in the results of your decisions and actions. In fact, one exercise will reveal much to you: Recall a particular act of your own, and ask yourself what you would feel if it had been done by an acquaintance of yours.

There is a lovely Spanish poem which addresses Jesus' point. It says if you have a beautiful garden and you want to know whether to invite a particular person into it, offer first a single petal from a flower and see what response is given. Then you will know whether your acquaintance can be a visitor who will love your garden — and you.

Look to God's Will   Jesus goes on in Matthew 7:21-23 to demolish stereotypes about "spiritual" people. At least he tried to demolish them. Unfortunately, they are still around and powerful. When we look for results in ourselves or others we tend to look for the external and obvious. But we must be cautious. Jesus says only one thing matters: Did you do the will of the Father? That is the only result he's interested in. Most of us are not in a position to decide whether another person does the will of the Father. Again, if we want to become peacemakers, children of God, we must look to ourselves.

Jesus indicates unmistakably that marvels are not enough, nor is verbal acknowledgment of him. It is not enough to call him Lord. Words can come too easily. Neither is it enough to do miraculous-looking deeds, like prophecy and exorcism, even in the name of Jesus. He is adamant. Only the will of the Father matters, and anything less is not recognized by Jesus.

What is the will of the Father? Look at the Beatitudes. See what he blesses. Note who sees him and who will be his children. The one who has walked this long path of blessedness, growing all the while and coming to profound peace and joy — that one fulfills the will of the Father.

This notion can be upsetting, because we think we know the will of God is hard and full of suffering. How peculiar that in the face of Easter morning we can *want* to stop at Good Friday afternoon! God wills us to be blessed, to be joyful. He wills us to be full of peace and to share that peace. Even while we want it, we fight it, for it seems to us too good to be true. So we strive for accomplishment instead, saying, let's *do* miracles. Let's heal and exorcise and prophesy. Certainly these are good! But the will of the Father goes deeper, to the peace and joy he wants for every heart, including yours and mine. If we become peace-filled, we will live in the kingdom of God (verse 21). If we are peace-filled, we already are in the kingdom where God is; and we cannot help exuding that peace to the world and to all our brothers and sisters.

So this Beatitude is the climax of the progression, isn't it? The peacemakers cannot give what they do not have. Those who have found peace within themselves can make peace, for they have seen God. All your experimentation and practice with the Beatitudes will lead to this final step: overflowing peace that is itself the kingdom of God. Now all you need to do is let it be, streaming easily from you to others. Be grateful, too, for this is the reality of heaven on earth. It is available to you as soon as you really want it.

9
Prepare for Trouble

**Blest are those persecuted for holiness' sake;
the reign of God is theirs (Matthew 5:10).**

The last three verses (Matthew 5:10-12) of the Beatitudes are strong statements about persecution. Together they seem to outweigh each of the other Beatitudes by sheer number of words. The reason for that may lie more in Matthew's emphasis than in Jesus'. Matthew's community was suffering when this Gospel was written. Although Christians were not actually hunted by the government, they were in some danger. Of course, their teachers in the faith had seen Jesus die on false charges. Now they were acclaiming him and were likely to be similarly treated. So the community needed reassurance about their fears of persecution.

What about us? Certainly verse 10 belongs to the pattern of the other Beatitudes. The kingdom is promised to those who suffer persecution because of their holiness. It won't be easy, Jesus says, because people resent those whose moral lives underline their own immorality.

The world is threatened by holiness and will often turn against it. Sometimes our toughest battle with that threat will be within ourselves. However we find it, Jesus does say that an unpleasant reaction to holiness can be anticipated from within ourselves or from outside sources. It will come; and its coming practically places the stamp of reality on our holiness. Would we dare say that if we do not experience some form of persecution, we are not holy enough to be noticed? Perhaps Jesus was merely realistic.

**Meaning of
Persecution** It is important to note, however, that "persecution" is not just *any* pain. When we experience pain we often find it so difficult that we cast about for any help we can find. Then we may remember these words and use them to provide hope for ourselves. But Jesus does not say that we are blessed because we suffer pain or because someone is merely nasty to us or hurts our feelings. The persecution which

brings bliss is of one kind only: that which comes because we are holy and dedicated to Jesus Christ.

Across the centuries since the time of Jesus some of his followers have experienced insult, slander, and even physical martyrdom because of their holiness, their allegiance to Jesus' way of life. Saints have even experienced it from other people who also claimed to be Jesus' followers, as when John of the Cross was thrown in an underground prison by members of his own religious order. But if today we look honestly at our pains and difficulties, we find few of them stemming from persecution.

Sometimes, people are hard on us because we have been hard on them. Sometimes, insults and slander are almost deserved. We have troubles and illness; and we suffer from ourselves, our families, friends, and enemies. But how often can we say it was our love for God which prompted our difficulties?

Years ago our society claimed an allegiance to Christianity. That day is past. Not only is our culture more pluralistic in religion, but the general societal values are far from Jesus' intention that we love each other more than anything or anyone except God. Our society simply does not function on love for one another. The violence in the streets is only a symptom of the lovelessness in our choices and our life-style. We may put comfort first, or independence or privacy or self-defense. As society continues to change, persecution may become part of our lives, but only if our lives are noticed because they differ from the bulk of society.

Many people today do not consider it intelligent to be Christian. Many Christians do not consider it quite bright to live as the Sermon on the Mount proposes. Others, both Christians and non-Christians, are searching eagerly for practical ways to live in love and in peace. Perhaps all who search must join together. Regardless, the search must first begin in our own souls.

Historically, it seems that persecution has almost always followed the world's recognition of holiness in its midst. There is hope for our present generation, however. A woman as obviously holy as Mother Teresa has been supported, accepted, even honored. If we grow together in love and peacemaking, persecution may not remain after all. Perhaps the day will come when holiness of life will be more supported than suspected by the majority. That will be the kingdom visible on earth.

Fitness for the Kingdom Meanwhile, although we may not be persecuted, it is necessary to recognize that those of us who want to live the Sermon on the Mount will not conform to the usual patterns of life dictated by our Western culture. Some of the hardest challenges may come from other Christians. Suddenly, we may not "fit" anymore if we take the Sermon seriously, even as an experiment. But we will find a freedom and happiness that was not ours before. That is certain. We will find deeper friendships with those who also are renewing their lives by Jesus' teaching. Like attracts like. If we are reaching out for love and peace and joy, those who are similarly seeking will find us. Then the beauty of our new life can be shared.

Still the discomfort we may feel when we don't fit can be nettlesome. Let's think about that for a few minutes. Why are we so uncomfortable when we are not like everyone else? Or not like the TV people? Or not like others — including our parents — have thought we should be? We tend only to approve of ourselves when we feel reassured by being approved or being like others. We feel a hidden fear that we are not really acceptable as we are, that we are not worthy of being alive and, especially, not worthy of being loved.

Yet, in some corner of ourselves we know it is foolish to depend on everyone else's opinion. Our fears often win out, though, and we let others determine what we feel, think, wear, and how we behave, even when we know there must be another way.

If we then consciously make a choice to live as Jesus taught in our Sermon, we may anticipate that we will be even farther from fitting into the society. Few make such a serious attempt with the Sermon on the Mount. Those few know happiness that no one else approaches. Because it is interior it is also not self-announcing. Yet, a person of peace is recognized, for we all need peace and it speaks to our longing when we meet someone who has it.

Few people set out specifically to become odd. Difference is a result of valuing something other than what our neighbors or the media value. When we choose to conform to the Sermon instead of society we are choosing one value over another. In that choice we experience differences from people who make other choices. In this case, those others will be in the majority.

How to Gain Peace

How do we handle the anxiety that nonconformity often produces in us? What can we do to keep our values and yet get rid of the fearfulness and sense of inadequacy that our neighbors may create in us? Here are a few suggestions:

First, remind yourself that the choice was yours. It does no good to say "I can't help it; I'm just like this." The choice was yours, you could "help it," and you are "like this" because you choose to be. Accept the responsibility for your choice, for with acceptance comes a delicious freedom. By taking control of your own situation, you become victor not victim. Hope is born in you the instant you can say, "I chose to be like I am." Try it and see!

Second, recall why you made the choice you did. If it was a deliberate choice (I want to live the Sermon) or a tough decision (I will learn to forgive), you will remember exactly your reasons and expectations. Recalling that you wanted peace will strengthen you and increase your resolve. Then compare — to see if the option of social conformity still seems attractive.

Third, ask whether it is really a problem to be somewhat unlike others. You have found peace. Can others' approval give you that? Are *you* comfortable with your choice, for yourself alone? If you are, then who is having the problem? It's the one who tries to make you feel odd — and remember that person also feels insecure and in need of approval. One who has been floating along not making the clear choices you have made will feel even less adequate in the face of your confidence. So now there is a special gift you can give to him or her: love and assistance from your own peaceful heart.

In offering your opponent love, you may experience two things. The chances are that your opponent will become your supporter or, at least, be more kindly disposed toward you. Few will resist the offer of love. Then, too, your own inner self will be stronger. Whatever the other person does, you have maintained your own integrity. Your self-respect will grow, and you will feel good about being who you are. After all, your aim is to become more like Jesus, so you will be doing what he did — showing love to the opposition. Even a step in that direction is exciting.

Finally, accept yourself. You now stand in a somewhat new position. You have made a choice, experienced difficulty, kept the choice as worthwhile, and loved those who did not offer you direct reward. You are a much stronger person for this experience. You can freely and justly pat yourself on the back. You have begun the transformation Paul speaks of: "Be transformed by the renewal of your mind" (Romans 12:2).

So enjoy yourself! Enjoy the uncluttered and shining happiness that is now your very own. Beside such a happy inner life persecution fades to insignificance. So does nonconformity. It's a great feeling. It belongs to you in God's kingdom. Some of you have found that already. Why not share your peace with those still reaching to find it?

10

Five Keys
to the
Kingdom

Our Father in heaven, hallowed be your name,
your kingdom come, your will be done
on earth as it is in heaven.
Give us today our daily bread,
and forgive us the wrong we have done
as we forgive those who wrong us.
Subject us not to the trial
but deliver us from the evil one
(Matthew 6:9-13).

These are the most familiar verses in the Sermon on the Mount. Jesus has been talking about prayer. He is objecting to multiplication of words for the sake of being heard (Matthew 6:7-8). It doesn't work that way, he says. You do not need to inform your Father of your needs. He knows them already. Then Jesus suggests a prayer pattern that we have all "rattled off" since we were old enough to memorize. We call it the "Our Father" or "Lord's Prayer." We usually say it by rote, both in public worship and private prayer. Yet, we could participate much more truly in the Lord's prayer.

Mere repetition of this prayer can hardly be Jesus' intention. That would be contrary to his great spirit of interiority about all of life. Still, there are some who feel that if they but repeat "his" words, they have captured the essence of the prayer. But they are not *praying* the "Lord's Prayer"; they are only *saying* it. Besides, we do not even know the exact words that Jesus used. (Matthew's English version of the prayer differs from that of Luke 11:2-4.) So, the power of the "Our Father" comes not from the words themselves but from the content of the words.

Jesus, then, is here concerned not just with a formula for prayer. He is giving us a design for our whole prayer life. If we view it that way, in the context of the Sermon, what do we find?

First, like the rest of the Sermon, the prayer is not just a statement of idealistic principles. It is to be practiced. Only if we take it as a practice-pattern for our prayer can we know how it will work in our lives. For living, formulas are never enough. Likewise in prayer, only practice makes changes in our lives.

The prayer has five main sections: a) address to the Father; b) prayer for the kingdom; c) request for today's necessities; d) openness to forgiveness; e) freedom from evil trial.

Let's look at each of these in turn.

Address to the Father　The Father and his holiness are the focus of the whole pattern. Jesus' prayer was addressed to the Father, and recognition was given to his holiness. That means the very name of the Father was to be held sacred. That one should not use God's name uselessly is not Jesus' point. Somewhere within each of us, sacredness, awe, wonder are still alive. These dispositions of our souls belong exclusively to the Father. He is our Creator and the Creator of all that is.

For our ongoing prayer life, this has several implications. Few of us are in immediate touch with awe or wonder. Our overblown ego reaches too quickly for control. If we are to pray with genuine, wondering reverence for the Father, we must settle down in quiet and openness before we even turn our hearts in God's direction. We give him our total readiness to hear his voice. We give him our total attention, calmly, expectantly. We do not clamor for his attention to our pleas. We rather attend to him. With our hearts more than with our words, we recognize that God is a loving Parent (like a father), that all ("our") people are his children, and that his holiness is beyond our grasp. He deserves our total attention and appreciation.

Take time for this, at least in your private prayer. Do not jump too quickly into words, whether of praise or memory or petition. There is time enough. Use a few minutes of it to let yourself sink serenely into the realization of divine awesomeness. Then, whatever expressions of appreciation, wonder, reverence come naturally can be freely used. Sometimes awe is stillness; sometimes it bubbles over in delight; sometimes it may demand words or dance or song. But don't rush. Slip quietly into awareness of majesty and unconditional love.

Prayer for the Kingdom Jesus' design for prayer moves from recognition of the awesomeness and beauty of the Father into a deep and moving desire for the fullness of his reign in every human life. In his ministry of preaching, teaching, healing, Jesus' whole thrust was toward the kingdom. The Sermon on the Mount is descriptive of kingdom life. This prayer pattern is explicitly concerned with the kingdom.

When you want the kingdom of God, you want it for all time, for every person, and especially for yourself. If you pray this prayer design with your life and not only with your mouth, the kingdom will become your single priority. Ponder that each time for awhile before you pray. God is love and beauty and healing, given in peace, the whole kingdom. Who could not want such a life for himself or herself, for all humans on the whole earth, for all future days? Just imagine what life would be like then! Focus on that. Plan on it. Depend on God for its realization. Pray continuously for the kingdom. Make it the initial thrust of all your prayer. Everything else you need or desire comes within the kingdom. Give it first place always and most especially when you pray.

Request for Today's Necessities In this section of the prayer Jesus mentions "daily bread." There is a scholarly question about how the earliest Christians understood this phrase, but for us it may refer to all everyday necessities: bodily necessities, emotional needs (*needs,* not every possible wish), spiritual fulfillment. Is Jesus here reminding the Father just in case he forgets? I think it's more like this: When we ask we usually are more open to receiving God's answer. If we affirm our dependence on God for the provision of our daily needs, we will be more expectant, regardless of the form God chooses to answer our prayer. As we expect more, we receive more fully.

Openness to Forgiveness The fourth section of Jesus' prayer pattern is really the main key to the kingdom. There is no way for God to reign securély throughout our lives unless we give and receive forgiveness. As we saw earlier, only when we forgive others can God's forgiveness have any effect in our own lives. We cannot pray for God's reign on the "earth as it is in heaven" unless we are ready always to forgive.

The most important single thing to understand about the Father is that he *is* Love. He loves each of us and all of us together without any conditions attached. He loves us whether we are doing his will or not, whether we are loving or not, whether we are seeking him or not. His love for us does not depend on us in any way. It depends only on him, on the quality of his own nature, apart from all the limitations that we alone want to attach to his loving us.

If we then pray for his reign in our lives and in the lives of all people, how can we resist forgiving everyone? How could we pray for fullness of love and refuse to forgive at the same time? To refuse forgiveness is to refuse to love someone we believe has injured us. To offer forgiveness is to love him or her without any reference to past failures, real or imagined. Actually, then, we *cannot* pray the "Our Father" with our lives unless we are ready to forgive all others freely and to forget that we were ever even hurt. We offer love because we offer love. Period. That is the way the Father loves all of us, even when we seem to hurt each other.

There is another difficulty for us in this section of the prayer, even if we are working at learning forgiveness. Do we really want God to forgive us exactly as we have forgiven others? How have we forgiven others? Freely and heartily? Easily and warmly? Immediately or only after long delay? Grudgingly? Or in some cases, not at all? How do we desire to experience God's forgiveness in our own lives? Here we are asking God to forgive us the way we forgive others. It is worth pondering, isn't it?

This prayer for openness to accept and give forgiveness will literally create the kingdom before your eyes. (This is most important for practicing the Sermon's principles.) Not the words alone — they have been said for centuries in the Christian world, and still wars and hatreds prevail. But if you adopt forgiveness as the basic ingredient of all your prayer life, your home and parish and neighborhood and friends will all sense the kingdom nearby, in you. And you yourself will know peace.

Suggested Since forgiveness is so necessary for the living of
Experiments the Sermon, you may need some added practices
in this area. Perhaps you will want to try one of the
following forms of experiment:

1. Each time you pray, whether at meals or in private meditation, make an act of forgiveness. Be specific. Name the person and the circumstance. You may be brief, but don't be general. "I forgive everybody" — these are only words. You need to put your heart firmly into your act of forgiveness. After you have practiced this for a time, you may add another specific person to forgive. Then you can happily give thanks to God for all the love filling your relationships.

Sometimes you feel you should forgive, but you don't really want to. Acknowledge that openly to God — he knows it anyway. But do not say words you don't mean, including the "Our Father." That only splits your intentions and allows you to deceive yourself. It isn't easy to repair habitually deceptive thinking. So, keep open and honest with God, especially on this key matter. But don't stop there. Continue your requests for help to become more willing to forgive and to learn how to do it freely.

2. Another form of practice may take place during the praying of the "Our Father" at Mass. If the words have become just that to you — mere words — pray them only mentally and listen to the sound of them from the rest of the community. This will give you the opportunity to concentrate more on the content than on the words themselves. You may feel a little odd, even left out, but you will become much more conscious of the importance of Jesus' central pattern for your prayer. You'll feel honest, too. Then return to verbalizing the prayer when you can do so truthfully.

3. You may want to use forgiveness in an examination of conscience, perhaps before you rest each night. Be careful that this review of your day does not become a listing of all who have made life difficult for you. Rather, approach it like this: "Was there a time today when I felt anger or anxiety? I now want to flood that time with a warm forgiving feeling for everyone (including myself) involved in the incident. I visualize Jesus there, spreading his

gentleness and acceptance. I join with him in that act." Then you will want to be still for a few minutes and let it happen within you. Finally, praise God for the love in your day!

If you do this daily — let's say for two weeks — you will discover that your need for review diminishes. You will respond with love more often during the day. You will be able, increasingly, to give thanks for the beautiful, peace-filled days you have, one after another after another.

Freedom from Evil Trial   The fifth section of the "Our Father" is a prayer for protection from evil trial. This phrase is variously translated, again because the original meaning is not altogether clear to linguists. Yet, it does acknowledge our human awareness of the danger to which we are susceptible. We go to the loving Father for protection from it.

We are not praying primarily never to be tempted, it would seem. For with temptation we can grow. We can use every such occasion to strengthen our desire to live totally in the kingdom. So, the protection sought here is from slipping unaware into the control of evil. The evil one can be so insidious that it is quite possible to become inwardly wrongheaded without knowing it. Circumstances may seem overwhelming; we may doubt the strength available to us, or for some other reason we do and say things that separate us from God. From this we all desire protection.

Such protection may come in the form of increased awareness of ourselves and our world. Or perhaps certain possibilities for evil don't materialize. Or we may be so joyful and faith-filled that trials don't have the power to upset us as they had before our practice in the Sermon. However God's assistance comes to our daily life, it communicates to us that our final place is with the Father. He will not allow us to remain separated from him forever, especially as we are seeking his reign over our lives. His love is never-ending and powerful. His protection from our tendency to slither into less than loving ways is an expression of his constant love. Count on it!

An effective way to incorporate this need in your prayer is by visualization. In quiet relaxation, see yourself safe. See yourself surrounded by strong arms or by a barrier of light or whatever symbolism is lively for you. Such "seeing" accepts the protection the Father always offers you. Gradually, you come to know that you are secure, and you know you can respond without fear in every situation.

To support your openness to God's protection, it may be helpful to reduce the attention you now give to frightening things. The media stories of horror, for example, do not contribute to your awareness of God's protective love. Conversations that begin "Isn't it awful what happened to . . ." also increase your level of fear. "Entertainment" — no matter how sophisticated — that is filled with human malice hammers away at your sense of security in God. Take a good look at this prayer phrase and then at your habits. Do they fit together? You may have to change something here before you can honestly pray for protection. Experiment with their reduction to see what happens.

You may also want to pray for the protection of others in the same way: visualizing them safe and surrounded by love and support. Then you can refrain from contributing to their fears, too. Several years ago an acquaintance called to warn me about incidents which had been happening in the general area where I lived. For 45 minutes she described all the lurid, fear-filled details, none of which were even potentially helpful to my safety. It was some time before I could leave the house without feeling apprehensive. Making a person afraid is never a favor. So, as you desire protection and pray for it, extend that same protection to others. Then your own will be more sure.

These suggestions may help make the "Our Father" a force in your prayer life rather than a formula repeated without real meaning. Your own experiments will open to you this design as a potent path to the kingdom. It will deepen your desire for God, increase your security in him in every way — materially, emotionally, relationally. It is a design for prayer that is sure to bring results, especially the peace that only the Father can offer through the Son in the kingdom. It is yours for the praying!

11

Practice Makes Perfect

The vision of the kingdom of God within our lives was the focus of Jesus' life and Resurrection. He lived it, demonstrated it, urged it, taught it. He fleshed it out in his own body, his own daily life. His words, his actions, his choices, his prayer all sprang from and pointed toward the kingdom of his Father, present and eternal.

Even his most immediate followers did not capture the fullness that Jesus assured them could be theirs. Their struggles were probably not so different from ours, despite the intervening centuries. We are very much like them. We hear, but not fully. We understand, and then find there is so much more to understand. We have information and tradition and scores of books, yet we know we need more. We are not always sure what that "more" might be. We cannot predict precisely what circumstances will come from our love for God. All our uncertainty was shared by those earliest disciples, too. Life is never really comfortable. However, if we don't ignore the discomfort, using it rather as a spur to growth, it can be helpful and creative. If we are uncertain about the kingdom, we can choose to respond by seeking and by experimenting, as this book has suggested.

The one thing we must not do — if we want results — is to keep the Sermon on the Mount in the realm of theory or "impossible idealism." Both of these charges have been leveled at the Sermon. If the Sermon is only a nebulous theory that does not work out in practice, then our Christian way of life is highly questionable. Maybe we ought to forget it. If the Sermon is a collection of nice ideals which all agree would be pleasant but impossible to reach, then there is not much point in any of us trying to live as Jesus taught.

Practice the Sermon　But if the Sermon is a pattern for peace, a guide to living joyfully in the kingdom of God, as I believe it to be, then all the idealism in the Church will not help us by itself. We will only know the truth as we begin to live it. All at once? That's not very realistic for most of us. We have to experiment. We have to practice.

In my college chemistry class the laboratory workbook told us exactly what steps to take and what results to expect. This was boring because the results were never surprises. In the laboratory of life, however, few of us will experiment with our whole being unless we have some idea of what to expect. Too much unknown is not usually very welcome in our hearts! So Matthew concludes the Sermon with Jesus' description of results: "Anyone who hears my words and puts them into practice is like the wise man who built his house on rock. When the rainy season set in, the torrents came and the winds blew and buffeted his house. It did not collapse; it had been solidly set on rock" (7:24-25). Those verses present a powerful image, don't they?

The results, he assures us, are total strength, total security, total peace. Even in the worst storms of life that may assail us, WE WILL STAND.

It may seem that there is much time and effort between where we are now and that complete security. But since we know that safety *is* the completion of our journey, we can begin in confidence, can't we?

Begin we must. We must begin to act, to experience the Sermon on the Mount. It is up to us. No one says we *have* to choose kingdom life. No one forces us to live according to this pattern. We are free to say no to any or all of it. But if we want to know whether it's true, action is the only way to find out.

It is like any other choice. Though we can choose as we wish, we cannot avoid the result that is attached to our choice. The results of choosing against the practice, the doing, of the Sermon are also graphically described in Matthew 7:26-27: "Anyone who hears my words but does not put them into practice is like the foolish man who built his house on sandy ground. The rains fell, the torrents came, the winds blew and lashed against his house. It collapsed under all this and was completely ruined." We can, therefore, do (or practice) the Sermon and be secure, or we can keep the Sermon a nice theory and be insecure. Viewed as Jesus viewed it, the choice is rather easy, isn't it?

The intriguing thing is that living the Sermon is easier than any other way. We have to resist only ego-habit. We cling to the old ways because they are familiar and somehow we've survived with them. But the actual energy expenditure of living the Sermon is far less than our usual societal way of life. I can't prove this. Only you can — by doing it.

It is completely up to you.

Share the Sermon   If you hesitate, maybe you feel the need to share your new project with other people. That is wise.

Sharing your thoughts with two or three or a group will prove very beneficial. You will expand each other's insights. Your blind spot will not be in the same place as your friends'. You will motivate each other. You will not all get discouraged or troubled at the same time. A group, practicing the Sermon together, is a wonderful experience.

If you, having read this book and done some of the experiments already, now want to continue your growth with a group, here are several ways to go about it:

1. You could send personal letters to people you know, inviting them to meet in your home. Explain the purpose of the gathering. Emphasize the necessity for commitment to the *practice* of the Sermon. Plan to limit the size of your group. It should be probably no fewer than four and not more than twelve. The ideal group would be nine or ten.

2. You may seek the assistance of your pastor. He may help you locate other interested persons. He (or one of his associates) might be glad to have you meet in the church or even to meet at your home. Don't let him take it over, though; and be sure he wants to practice also. Keep the number of participants small, and don't let this become a lecture series! All members need to remain close to the daily experiment.

3. You may find just the right people in an already existing prayer group. When these groups need revitalization, a turn to the Sermon might be exactly right. If the prayer group is too large, an

announcement in the group might be enough to gather those who are seriously interested.

4. Other groups already established (Sodalities or Guilds, for example) may also provide interested people. If the whole organization wants to try the Sermon, divide the participants into small Practice Groups. Don't let the size of an already established group dictate the size of the Sermon group. Keep it small.

5. During the sessions themselves stay close to the Sermon itself and to your daily practice and daily prayer. This book is only a starter. It is certainly not the last word on the Sermon for anyone, even the writer! Use it as long as it is practical enough to keep you practicing. Otherwise, live beyond it.

If you have practiced your way through this book, you already have many new insights. They come from the Spirit almost the instant you are actively willing to let them in. Share them with others as they come. But I need not tell you, you have just begun. So, turn right around and start again from the beginning. You may want to review and reuse the suggestions of this book. You may want to go straight to the Sermon as Matthew has it. You may want to search out other books or create your own approach. The method doesn't matter much. What does matter is that you keep growing in your practice of the Sermon.

Chapters 5, 6, and 7 of Matthew contain Jesus' design for peace in our lives. Let's quit looking everywhere else for things and circumstances to bring us joy. Let's turn instead to the pattern created by the One who created life itself. Then we know for certain that the outcome can be only profound peace and spontaneous joy in the daily life of God's kingdom.